# BACK ON TRACK

Happy Birthday Mate!

Dear Johnny,

I thank God that He + c loved me to be a part of your spiritual journey. A walk filled w/ups & downs, highs & lows, victories & defeat - through it all, God loves, believes & refines. May this book help during times of drifting. Pointing you back to times of refreshing (Acts 3:20).

# BACK ON TRACK

## A 40-DAY JOURNEY
## TO SPIRITUAL RENEWAL

# JIMMY ALLEN

**DPI**
DISCIPLESHIP
PUBLICATIONS
INTERNATIONAL

www.dpibooks.org

**Back on Track**

Cover Design: Brian Branch


ISBN: 978-1-57782-300-1

To my girls…

I have never questioned why God gave me you. It is clear. I have never once wanted to swap you for fellas. You are the sparkle in my eye. You have taught me more about God the Father than you will ever know.

Kelsey, I don't know a lot about parenting, but I do tell people get the first one to head in the right direction and hopefully the rest will follow. You are the heart of our family. Your beautiful voice and smile brighten my day.

Jenna, the middle child has a special place. You always got hand-me-downs but you also constantly lifted your sisters and parents up. You are the zeal in our family. Though early on I was not looking for a strong-willed child, your energy channeled to do right inspires me consistently.

Sarah, it is tough to be the youngest. Mom and I were a bit tired by the time you came along. Though you now have to travel with us solo, your willingness to chart your own course and make life the best it can be is fun to watch. You are the competitor in our family. Your intense focus on excellence in athletics, AP courses, and walking with God is amazing.

Anita, you are the love of my life. Your beauty still captivates me. You are our family. I am sure our family would not survive a week without you. Thanks for moving across the country, making New England your home, and loving Connecticut as your own. I want and need no other partner.

I don't cry often, as you know. I get teary as I type this because you all move me emotionally like virtually nothing else does. I love you all very, very much. You really are my heroes.

# CONTENTS

## My God

## My Head

## My Heart

# My Hands

# My Feet

# My Lips

# ABOUT THIS BOOK

## A NOTE FROM THE PUBLISHER
## TAKE THE 40-DAY JOURNEY TO SPIRITUAL RENEWAL

> "Most of us don't dramatically dart away, but we sure do drift. Then there comes a day when we say, 'How did I end up here?' This book is an effort to help some find the way back to the Father. But beyond that, it is an attempt to help us all reignite our passions, retrofit our plans and return whole-heartedly to the gospel train of God's purposes."
> —from the Introduction

This is a book to help individual Christians, small groups and whole congregations get back on track for God.

In a writing style that is vulnerable, humorous, challenging and fresh, Jimmy Allen, a church leader for more than twenty-five years, sets the book up in the following way:

- Six sections of overall focus: My God, My Head, My Heart, My Hands, My Feet, My Lips
- An introduction and 24 chapters to be spaced out in 40 daily readings
- "Getting Back on Track" follow-up questions at the end of each reading
- Space to write responses in the book

Forty days—a very biblical time frame to change, motivate and empower us to move forward. We would hate for anyone to miss the train!

This is not a gimmick and not just a program—it is an honest attempt to help individuals and churches be what we really in our heart of hearts want to be. (A special packet of support material is available for church leaders.)

> "So...All Aboard! Trains can be tied to trauma. But even wreckage can be recreated. What is cold can be reheated. What is far can be brought near. What is lost can be found. What is dead can become alive again."—from the Introduction

# DAY 1
# INTRODUCTION

## Back on Track

On October 23, 2009, in Mumbai, India, a train rolled comfortably down the tracks. It was on its usual passenger run. However, this day was to be anything but usual. At approximately 10:45 AM, a support girder holding up the pedestrian bridge above the train gave way causing a water pipe and a large cement block to fall at exactly the wrong time. Three people were killed in the carnage that resulted, including the engineer, and many others were injured. The train derailed. Panic and chaos ensued.

The nine-car train did not set out to crash that day. But it did. Lives were lost. Property was destroyed. A beautiful day was ruined for many.

Has the sky ever fallen on you? Has your life ever gotten off track? Have you ever felt like major damage was going on all around? You didn't intend for it to happen. However, spiritual train wrecks take place in people's lives all the time. Sadly, I get a front row seat for these too often.

Do you know what the Indians did in the face of the Thane-Kopri bridge collapse? No, this accident didn't happen in the U.S. or Canada, and the clean-up didn't take place within the next few days. But after a while, in this third world country, the Central Railway Company sent the gnarled, steel chamber of death to a Matunga workshop.

At the workshop, the former nine-car train was transformed. Piece by piece it was put back together—some additions here; deletions there. A new driver's coach was put in place. Cables and wires reconnected cars to each other. And a crushed piece of junk was changed to a twelve-car, new-and-improved, retrofitted train. In March of 2010, the revitalized train went back on the tracks.

How does abandoned scrap become a sleek and speedy means of travel? How does a life off course get back to where it once was and even beyond? David knows—from writing Psalms to committing sins to being like God is his spiritual roller-coaster of a tale. The prodigal son might have some thoughts—from member of the family to the far country and home to Dad's pad again.

Many of you reading this book may not have experienced an extreme story of derailment. But we can all relate to getting off track and the damage it causes. It hardens our hearts. It wastes our time. It distances us in relationships—with God and others.

Most of us don't dramatically dart away, but we sure do drift. Then there comes a day when we say, "How did I end up here?" This book is an effort to help some find the way back to the Father. But beyond that, it is an attempt to help us all reignite our passions, retrofit our plans and return wholeheartedly to the gospel train of God's purposes.

## Forty Days

For the next forty days, I invite you to join me (okay, it's really for a lifetime but that sounds too daunting right now). When I began this book, I was going to make this a thirty-day study. But the more I thought about it, the more I realized that "forty days" just kept coming up over and over in the Bible. It rained for forty days in the story of Noah and the flood (Genesis 7:12). Moses went on the mountain with God twice for this distinct time period (Exodus 24:18, 34:28). The twelve spies also explored the Promised Land for forty days (Numbers 13:25). And then there was Jesus. God's one and only Son fasted for forty days (Matthew 4:1–2) and appeared following his resurrection to his followers for forty days as well (Acts 1:3). If forty was "God's number," I decided that would take precedence over my month of thirty.

Some days, I am asking you to read one lesson and answer the questions. On most sections, you have two days. I don't want you to rush through. I want you to get God's message planted deeply in your heart.

So, let's dive into a study of God's word and his principles in the hopes of taking steps toward Jesus, tying in to his Holy Spirit and getting back on track again.

## Six Areas of Devotion

As we enter into this series, we are going to divide our study into six categories: My God, My Head, My Heart, My Hands, My Feet and My Lips. These areas will represent who God is and everything that we are. In other words, God is sovereign and he wants our mind, our emotions and passions, our actions and our words.

Virtually everyone that I know does better in one or two of these spiritual-life areas than in others. However, God wants it all. If you are a thinker, praise God. Lord knows we need more of those. But don't forget to speak up. Are you a doer? Wonderful! Most of us are way too happy sitting around watching TV. But don't leave your heart behind. God deserves our best. Let's go after "doing all things well" (Mark 7:37) just like our Savior.

So...All Aboard! Trains can be tied to trauma. But even wreckage can be re-created. What is cold can be reheated. What is far can be brought near. What is lost can be found. What is dead can become alive again.

There have been a few songs sung through the years entitled "The Gospel Train." However, the one that moves me the most was sung by slaves years ago and served as code language for the Underground Railroad.

The lyrics go like this:

> *The Gospel train's a comin'*
> *I hear it just at hand*
> *I hear the car wheel rumblin'*
> *And rollin' through the land*
> *I hear the train a comin'*
> *She's comin' round the curve*
> *She's loosened all her steam and brakes*
> *And strainin' every nerve*
> *The fare is cheap and all can go*
> *The rich and poor are there*
> *No second class aboard this train*
> *No difference in the fare*
>
> *CHORUS*
> *Get on board little children*
> *Get on board little children*
> *Get on board little children*
> *There's room for many more*

So, I'll say it again…last call: All Aboard!

1. What has been the worst "train wreck" day of your life? Your past month?

2. What event(s) has most thrown you off spiritually?

3. What damage or repercussions have you seen in your spiritual life when you have gotten off track?

4. What can you begin to do today to make steps toward getting back on track?

# MY GOD

# DAY 2
# UNDRAGONED

## You Undress Me

So he said to me, "This is the word of the LORD to Zerubbabel: 'Not by might nor by power, but by my Spirit,' says the LORD Almighty."

Zechariah 4:6

"God, to me, it seems, is a verb, not a noun."

—Richard Fuller

In this book we will talk about what you and I can do to relight the spiritual fervor in our hearts. That's fine. However, you and I can never do this "Jesus thing." It is beyond us. It is impossible. On our own power, that is.

In *The Voyage of the Dawn Treader*, one of the *Chronicles of Narnia* movies, there is a brief scene where a dragon turns back into a boy. I have heard from others that in the book this story is expanded.

Apparently, this snotty-nosed and unliked kid, Eustace, turned into a dragon because he ended up the way he acted—pretty dastardly. At first, the dragon thing was kind of cool for Eustace because he could scare people and breathe fire. However, eventually this thrill left him as he dealt with fear and loneliness.

Finally, in a rare moment of humility, Eustace, in his dragon form, followed Aslan (the lion and Jesus figure) to a pool. There,

Aslan told Eustace that he could not "undragon" himself. Aslan said, "I must undress you." Though Eustace had tried to scrape his scales off many times, try as he might, more layers of scales just kept popping up. It was only when the dragon allowed Aslan to undress him that he went under the water of the pool and came up again as Eustace, the boy.

We all have a lot of undragoning that we must go through.

**Be Filled with the Spirit**

In Ephesians 5:18, the apostle Paul writes of a very interesting contrast. He begins by saying, "Do not get drunk on wine." I'm guessing he was speaking from experience. I'm also guessing that most people who are reading this have either been drunk themselves or have seen others drunk. Is drunkenness something that is easy to hide? No way! It can be detected very easily. First you get the wine, and then the wine gets you.

The last phrase of this verse is, "Instead, be filled with the Spirit." In context, he seems to be saying, "Be drunk on the Holy Spirit of God versus the unholy spirit of wine." Why? Because when you are filled with the Spirit, it also changes everything! If you are filled with the Spirit, it is noticeable. People should be saying, "Wow. He is on something. I am not sure what she did, but that lady is so different." Are you? Is anyone saying that?

We need to change. We must get closer to God. That starts with a revival of the Holy Spirit in our life. Do we quench the Spirit or put out his fire (1 Thessalonians 5:19)? Other names for the Spirit are helpful in this discussion. God gave us a Counselor (John 16:7) because we need counsel. Our wisdom alone doesn't cut it.

God placed within the Christian a helper (John 14:26 NASV) because we have to have help!

Our Father made sure we had a comforter (John 14:16 KJV). Why? Certainly for comfort, but this also implies that we are not comfortable already. Unless I am living radically and on-the-edge for Christ, I have no real need to be comforted. In the first century, Christ-followers were hated, persecuted and killed for their faith. They had to have a comforter to make it through. Do I have to have him too?

In John 16:7, Jesus actually told his twelve apostles that it would be better for them when he left. He said that the Holy Spirit would live within them, while he had only walked beside them. Do you believe that? I often think how great it would be to have Jesus physically around. He himself says that I am better off with the Holy Spirit within than even a flesh-and-blood Savior beside. You have plenty of power at your disposal to be a spiritual man or woman.

Go to God. Let him undragon you.

## Power to Change

In Acts 2, the Holy Spirit's arrival changed everything. Cowering disciples in an upper room fearing for their lives became bold proclaimers of truth once the Holy Spirit entered the picture. Three thousand were baptized in a day, and things didn't stop at Pentecost. In Acts 4:29–31, the Holy Spirit showed up again; a building was shaken and courage continued. The book of Acts is living testimony to a people who were changed not by their own might or power but by the Spirit of our omnipotent God.

I am a believer. I come and go on this conviction, sadly. But today I am definitely a believer. In the past couple of months I have witnessed men and women of average strength and above-average sinfulness leaving behind sexual addictions, smoking habits of many years, alcohol problems, eating fetishes, rebellious teen behavior and more. None of them started off even thinking they could be different.

If you want to change, it starts with Jesus. Acts 4:13 says,

> When they saw the courage of Peter and John and
> realized that they were unschooled and ordinary
> men, they were astonished and they took note that
> these men had been with Jesus.

They didn't notice their great baritone singing voices, eloquent sermons, limitless potential and talents...but they realized that these disciples were who they were because of Christ.

Let's not start this book, this day or this second without him. So as we begin, let's pray.

*Dear Lord, undragon us. Awaken your Spirit in us mightily. Get our fruit out of the way and put yours in. Do what only you can do in our lives. We believe. Help our unbelief. In your amazing Son's name we pray. Amen.*

1. What dragon-like characteristics do you naturally exhibit?

2. Write down everything you know about the Holy Spirit.

3. How have you seen the Holy Spirit change your life in the past and in the present?

4. How can you tap into God's power today and see his strength unleashed in your life?

# DAY 3

# ASTRONOMICAL

## Googling God

"But will God really dwell on earth? The heavens, even the highest heaven, cannot contain you. How much less this temple I have built."

1 Kings 8:27

"Astronomy compels the soul to look upwards and leads us from this world to another."—Plato

Have you ever typed the words "the universe" into a search engine?

How about "Hubble Telescope," "galaxies," or "NASA"? I did that this past week. All kinds of videos, pictures and information came flooding into my little computer world...and it showed me a gigantic, enormous, eternal, immeasurable, astronomical God.

Let's start really small with a Milky Way Galaxy fact: The sun is 93 million miles away from earth. I recently drove to Arkansas and back with my family. That is about 1300 miles and 22 hours one way. It seems like a long, long, long drive. That is a blink of the eye compared to 93 million miles. By the way, I'm not complaining about the sun's distance. I don't want that incendiary, ferocious, intense ball of fire coming in at approximately 10,000 degrees Fahrenheit any closer to me than it already is (or any further away, for that matter—I kinda like God's placement).

Ninety three million miles in space is like an inch in comparison to the size of the unending and immense universe we are a part of. Our single galaxy is 100,000 light years across. Light travels at 186,000 miles per second.

Did you get that?

Per *second*! That is 5.88 trillion miles in a year. Hop on that rocking ray and you can get across a fairly small portion of our universe in 100,000 years!

If a trip to the sun is an inch, then a jaunt across the Milky Way would be a foot. Now, let's try a mile or two. I recently read that if an auditorium the size of Royal Albert Hall in London (which can hold 5500+) were filled with frozen peas, that would be the estimated number of galaxies in the solar system.

What?

Millions of stars (some larger and some smaller than our sun) fill each galaxy. Thousands of galaxies fill our known universe (think of what is still unknown!). Billions of light years stretch from east to west and north to south just from what we have found so far. By the way, I am using the word "we" in the previous sentence very loosely.

Psalm 147:4 says, "He determines the number of the stars and calls them each by name." Do you think God can remember your name? Psalm 108:4 states, "For great is your love, higher than the heavens." Do you think the Creator loves you?

The Living Bible uses these words in Isaiah 48:13: "It was my hand that laid the foundations of the earth; the palm of my right hand spread out the heavens; I spoke and it came into being." Did our Father just say that he put the stars in his palm and scattered them out?

If the known universe is 14 billion light years across (with es-
timates up to 20 billion) and God holds all that in the palm of
his hand—how big does that make the author of life?

How about this one?

Jeremiah 32:17 gushes, "Ah, Sovereign Lord, you have made the
heavens and earth by your great power and outstretched arm.
Nothing is too hard for you."

Will it be too hard for God to pull you back in close to himself? Is it too difficult for Christ (a co-creator by the way—
Colossians 1:15–17) to restore you? Can he handle your
addiction? Your circumstances? Your problems?

In Job 25, Bildad the Shuhite stands startled in front of God's
dominion and awe, as the One who ordered the heights in the
heaven. He closes out the chapter by calling mankind nothing
more than maggots and worms.

David said it this way in one of his moving writings,
Psalm 8:3–4,

> When I consider your heavens,
>     the work of your fingers,
> the moon and the stars,
>     which you have set in place,
> what is man that you are mindful of him,
>     the son of man that you care for him?

God is **HUGE** and we are TINY.

## A Powerful and Caring God

He wants to help. He does care. He will come to our aid. Anything is possible. In fact, all is probable with the Almighty.

Worm-like creatures (caterpillars) can become butterflies. The Romans 12:1–2 transformation passage (*metamorphosis* in the Greek) says God can take us from the ooze of the mud to the ozone of the universe.

In Philippians 2:13, the Bible says that God works in you for his purpose. He can. He will. He does.

## From God's Perspective

When I was small, a twenty-year-old African man traveled to our small city to play basketball for the local college team. He was over seven feet tall. I believe he could dunk a basketball on his tip toes. His name was Himan. I'm not sure about the spelling of that. I'm also not sure if it was a name or a nickname. He was a high man and when I saw him, I would say, "Hi!... Oh, Man."

One day, Himan put me on his shoulders and carried me up and down Magnolia Drive. I was freaked out. I had never seen life from that point of view. It was scary for sure, but also exhilarating and empowering.

What if we were to take a piggy back ride on God? What if we took a lift on his broad shoulders? It would definitely change our perspective and our lives.

Google God. Then choose God. Again. He is astronomical.

## GETTING BACK ON TRACK

1. From what you know about the solar systems and space, take a few moments to contemplate how big God is. Now try to describe that immensity.

2. If you could keep a clear view of an astronomical God in the forefront of your mind, how would that affect your faith?

3. If you viewed your life from God's perspective, what might you see that you don't now see?

4. List three things that a huge God could help do in your life and circumstances this year.

# DAY 4

# FEAR

## On Getting Old

Be happy, young man, while you are young,
  and let your heart give you joy in the days of
    your youth.
Follow the ways of your heart
  and whatever your eyes see,
but know that for all these things
  God will bring you to judgment.

Ecclesiastes 11:9

"A man is not old until regrets take the place of dreams."—John Barrymore

We studied the book of Ecclesiastes for six months last year in our congregation. We went verse by verse. The book of Ecclesiastes is very depressing, especially if you go verse by verse. Lots of people told me near the end that they were very depressed. I don't know if that was really good preaching or really bad. At the end of our study, everyone applauded. I'm not sure if that was because they really liked the final lesson or were just glad it was over. Solomon, the author and richest, most powerful man on the planet at the time really needed some help or medication or something.

Do you know what "Ecclesiastes" means? Here's a hint. It comes from a similar Greek root word we are more familiar with: *ecclesia*. This means "the called out" or "congregation" and was eventually translated "church" in most English versions. Apparently, Solomon is "the preacher" to the assembly. I guess that means that preachers really can cause depression. Okay, you already knew that. We'll move on.

## The Coming of Old Age

At the close of the seemingly endless, utter despondency is Ecclesiastes 12. In the past, I have just read verses 1 and 2 about "remembering your Creator in the days of your youth" and then skipped to the conclusion. If you go verse by verse, you can't skip like that (unfortunately).

In verses 2–7 there is a graphic, grotesque and captivating view of old age. I now believe it to be the key section in this intense book. I've never seen it before. I think someone snuck it in there late in 2008 or so.

It says that days are coming when the sun, moon and stars grow dark (eyesight fades); when the keepers of the house tremble (limbs shake); when strong men stoop (bent backs); when the grinders cease because they are few (lose your teeth); when the sound of grinding fades (lose your hearing); when men rise at the sound of birds (don't sleep well); when men are afraid of heights and other dangers (paranoia and vulnerability); when the almond tree blossoms (gray hair); when the grasshopper drags himself along (joints are pained); and when desire is no longer stirred (I know what I'm thinking, but I'll let you try your own exegesis on this one).

## Looking Back with Regret

I am convinced that Solomon wrote the most backboard screeching, woe-is-me letter ever because he got old, started falling apart and looked back at his life with complete regret. He pulled out his pen and screamed, "Don't do what I did!"

There is only one problem with this. Pretty much all of Israel had been doing exactly what he did for years. He was the poster boy for money, position, power, prestige, fashion (Matthew 6:29) and who-you-want-to-be-when-you-grow-up. Thousands had followed this man to the precipice. And most were about to fall over the cliff.

Finally Solomon, the Teacher, makes sense in verses 13–14 as he says,

> Now all has been heard;
>> here is the conclusion of the matter.
> Fear God and keep his commandments,
>> for this is the whole duty of man.
> For God will bring every deed into judgment,
>> including every hidden thing,
>> whether it is good or evil.

Perhaps you have heard before that the original Hebrew apparently knocks out the word "duty" in this passage and says that fearing God and keeping his commands "is the whole of man." God's word says that it all, the "whole," can be summed up in fearing God.

This message doesn't sell in Christian bookstores today. Love, grace and forgiveness are repackaged in a million ways while sin, judgment and hell are nowhere to be found (except in the Bibles over in the next section). I am a big fan of love, grace and forgiveness and am hoping Solomon found all three in the final days of his life. But that is not what he shared in his last words. He said, "Fear God."

**Fear God**

We drift away and walk away from God because we do not fear or follow the One who created us. If we did, we would go nowhere ever. We would stick adhesively to him day and night. We would read, fast, pray, mourn and obey (keep his commands).

Ecclesiastes does not close out with, "And they all lived happily ever after." It says, "God will bring every deed into judgment." He mentions that this will include even the things you didn't get caught doing by others down here (hidden things).

Fear God. I have heard numerous people try to tell me that this doesn't mean "fear." It means "respect," "admire" or "hold in high regard." Thanks for your thoughts. I'm going to stick with the novel concept that "fear" means "fear," especially when in the context of God bringing everyone into judgment.

Revere his name. Fall down at his feet where you belong. Tremble. Cry. Shake and quake in your boots.

I'll tell you something you really don't want to know right now. I turned fifty this past year and, to celebrate, had my first colonoscopy ever. I remember thirty. That didn't seem old. I recall forty. I don't remember it being too bad. At fifty, they start sending stuff down you in ways things are not meant to be going down and fishing around for something. Fifty all of a sudden started feeling old. My back hurts. My knees creak. My stomach makes embarrassing gurgling noises at inopportune times.

I have not lived anywhere near a perfect life. But I can honestly say in my years of declining health (I've started early with diminished sight and hearing and tooth decay), I don't look back with massive regrets. I have been through some challenging times. I have certainly sinned and hurt people. But by and large, I have tried to have a relationship with God for most of my days. I have attempted to love people.

I probably shouldn't admit it because some might accuse me of being too ultra Paul-like spiritual, but I actually look forward to going to heaven more and more every day. As body parts come and go, sag and snap, rise and fall in mostly the exact opposite directions than I would want; I don't look back with depression at the years.

Fear God. One of my all-time favorite verses closes with this question, "But what will you do in the end?" (Jeremiah 5:31). Too many take salvation way too lightly. It is the biggest deal of all. We can't mock God. We will not manipulate the Judge. Neither you nor I will talk our way around anything.

Fear God. Revere his name. Do it now, before your eyes and ears go and your hair turns gray. And if they already have, you can still decide to revere his name. Come back in close to him. You will be eternally thankful that you did. One of life's greatest gifts at the end of the road is no regrets.

## GETTING BACK ON TRACK

1. What are you afraid of? Why?

2. What does it mean to you to fear God?

3. How do you feel about growing older? Why?

4. What regrets do you have? Is there a way to deal with them? Will you? When and how?

# MY HEAD

# DAY 5
# TRUST

## Become a Bird Watcher

"Behold the fowls of the air: for they sow not, neither do they reap, nor gather into barns; yet your heavenly Father feedeth them. Are ye not much better than they?"

Matthew 6:26 (KJV)

"A bird does not sing because it has an answer. It sings because it has a song."—Chinese Proverb

People had traveled for miles under the toasty Palestinian sun. They were tired and hungry, but wanted to listen to this new teacher who was the talk of Galilee. They had loads of problems in their Roman-oppressed, third-world country. Where would the next meal come from? How could their children make it through difficult times? With sickness so widespread, how could they and their loved ones even survive?

And then the radical rabbi said, "Look at the birds."

Now, my reaction to that would have been a foul attitude and a smart-aleck comment: "I can look at fowls in my own back yard. I didn't have to come all the way out here to do that."

In twenty-first century America, we get all caught up in paying the mortgage, making the sport's team or looking for a mate. We don't have time to slow down and check out animals! We have important things to tend to. Very few people are out sight-seeing for sparrows these days.

But right in the middle of his longest sermon ever recorded, Jesus called people to the first ever bird watching society meeting. And, in essence, he said…Birds don't have retirement plans or great resumes. Fowls don't fly around with Daytimers and degrees. Eagles are elegant, but don't they kick their young out of the nest (sounds like bad parenting to me)? Robins just up and fly south for awhile when the mood hits them without saying "goodbye" to all of their friends. Blue jays eat worms. Vultures scavenge, and I think they have been known to even eat rocks.

But God the Creator takes care of literally thousands of birds. Big ones. Small ones. Old ones. Young ones. Yellow ones. Black ones. And they all have no choice but to trust him for their food, shelter and survival.

Then the Jewish teacher said in his sermon, in the form of a question, that we are worth more than a fowl. We're better than birds. We even rate above a flower and a blade or two of grass, he added later.

## Your Dad Is Watching

Many years ago, our family stayed in a cabin in Alabama for a few days. My youngest daughter, Sarah, a baby at the time, fell under the muddy waters in a nearby lake for a scary couple of seconds while we were enjoying a swim. I was watching her and was able to grab her very quickly, and though she sputtered and spewed for a while, she was ultimately fine. Okay, in all honesty, I lost "watching privileges" for the rest of the trip.

This sad tale is told in our household often. But the truth of that story is that Dad was always nearby. I had my eye on her. I was watching. She wasn't going to drown. And somehow in my weakness, I get to be the hero today for saving my daughter's life.

It seems to me that way too many of us freak out constantly as we scream about our demise, death and destruction. Every wind that blows causes drama and trauma. Anxiety, stress and worry consume us, and we often drag in everyone close by. "I'm drowning, I'm drowning" is our daily refrain.

Can I let you in on a little secret? Your dad is watching. You are safe with him. Your almighty, loving Father has had his eye on you the whole time. His arms are strong enough to save.

And so when the apostle says in 1 Peter 5:7, "Cast all your anxiety on him because he cares for you," don't you think we should believe him? What if we actually tried this? And prayed. And pictured God with us daily. Because he is. And found peace. I mean an actual put-into-practice peace that passes understanding (Philippians 4:7).

In our congregation not too long ago, we each wrote down our worries on an index card. Of course, the cards weren't big enough, so we allowed people to just put etc. at the bottom. We had everything imaginable on those pieces of paper. There were finances, heart palpitations, children issues, singles' struggles, car problems, bad teachers, fashion-challenged parents, no job, bad job, a world at war—and there was even *worry*! Yes, we can even get all stirred up worrying because we worry too much and know God doesn't want that.

Thankfully, after all the writing, we talked about really laying all of our anxieties down at the foot of the cross. We decided to walk up to a cross on stage and leave our cards there as a video played. But more than a card exercise, we said we would leave our worries and really trust our dad one day at a time. Because we do agree with Jesus, who in that same sermon on the mountain said, "Each day has enough trouble of its own."

So your assignment today is to go bird watching. Yes, spend a few minutes and watch some type of fowl. Then get up and trust that the bird maker will take care of you too. Hey, who knows, if you leave the worry behind, you might even feel like flying as well.

## GETTING BACK ON TRACK

1. What are the main things you worry about?

2. What can you learn from bird watching Bible style?

3. Do you think a loving, watching Father would let you drown in your pool of financial, relational or emotional problems? Why or why not?

4. Write out your "worry card." Make a cross (can be of two toothpicks, pencils or larger). Have a brief ceremony (prayer, song and announcements if you must). Leave your card and anxieties behind at the foot of the cross. Did you really? How will this change your week and life ahead?

# DAYS 6 & 7
# COMMITMENT

## Be Salty Salt

"What good will it be for a man if he gains the whole world, yet forfeits his soul? Or what can a man give in exchange for his soul?"

Matthew 16:26

"Anyone can dabble, but once you've made that commitment, your blood has that particular thing in it, and it's very hard for people to stop you."

—Bill Cosby

Our "Neighbor Day" Sunday service to kick off the new year was approaching. I had a thought: "What if Jesus were preaching this upcoming Sunday? What would he say?" It wasn't the first time that thought has crossed my mind. It's a good question for a preacher, right? But then an additional thought crossed my brain that would not allow me to sleep well that night. It was, "What did Jesus say to large crowds back in his day? When the multitudes came, what was his first-century message?"

I tossed and turned that evening. I kind of knew what was coming and was afraid I was going to have to preach it that week. The next day I studied out the texts that mention Jesus preaching to large crowds. First, on several occasions he healed the sick, fed the hungry or just "met needs" in our terminology. But that wasn't his preaching. I had committed to check out his sermon content.

## Jesus' Sermons to the Crowds

I started with the Sermon on the Mount. Go read it in Matthew 5–7, and you'll find one of the most inspiring, challenging and radical lessons ever. That, by itself, is a book or two of thoughts.

Next I was directed to Mark 10:1 and following. In front of this crowd of people, Jesus discoursed on "divorce." That is one intense topic. I rarely speak on that in depth, and when I do it is not for a neighbor-day crowd.

Then I landed on Luke 8:4–8, the Parable of the Soils. Now first you have to imagine a culture in which people walked long distances from surrounding towns to hear this new teacher. They could easily have spent hours traveling to the sermon site. Upon arrival, this large agricultural crowd heard from the teacher that a farmer threw seed on a path, and it didn't grow. He then threw seed on ground with rocks and thorns, and that didn't work out too well. When he finally threw seed on good soil, things went better. And then Jesus stopped.

Well, he didn't quit quite yet. He added the phrase, "He who has ears, let him hear." My rendition of that is, "Figure this out if you can."

Hold on. I'm not a farmer, and even I know that seed on a road isn't going to work. So the apostles, who had probably been inviting all these folks to their neighbor day, ran up to Jesus and said, "What's the deal with that?"

Christ said, in essence, "I'm so glad you asked. That's what I want. I want people to come search me out after the teaching and want to know more. In fact, I saw this huge gathering and wanted to tell them this parable mainly to confuse them."

What? Jesus didn't do that, did he? I've heard my whole life that Christ taught in parables to help people understand. But here he is in Luke 8:10 saying he speaks in parables so that "though seeing they may not see; though hearing, they may not understand." I repeat, in plain English, whether you like it or not—that means he was trying to confuse people.

It seems that my Savior wanted people to scratch their heads and show a little more gumption beyond being entertained by a speech. He wanted to be chased down. He wanted to know if they would come looking for more.

And most people didn't.

## Committed Love

But we are really only getting started. In Luke 14:25–35, the Son of God encountered another large crowd. Perhaps he polled the apostles on sermon ideas. John may have suggested "Friendship from the Book of Proverbs" and Andrew probably thought "The Joy of Jesus" was catchy. Instead their Lord decided upon this lengthy title, "You have to hate your father, mother, yourself, everyone else and everything else if you want to follow me." He was talking about committed love.

If I can take you to the end of this speech, look more closely at verses 34–35,

> "Salt is good, but if it loses its saltiness, how can it be made salty again? It is fit neither for the soil nor for the manure pile; it is thrown out. He who has ears to hear, let him hear."

In the aforementioned Sermon on the Mount, Christ had called his followers to be salt. Here he says that if the salt is unsalty, it isn't even fit for the manure pile. I think he just said that if we aren't totally committed to him, we are worse than poop. Not much can be thrown on manure and ruin it! But apparently people who call themselves salt without being salt are just that. And then Jesus closes with that ever-present nifty phrase about ears, meaning "Figure this out if you can."

## More Confusion?

Oh no, we are not done yet. You have to read John 6 to believe it. At the crescendo of this seminar keynote address to the masses, Jesus said, "I tell you the truth, unless you eat the flesh of the Son of Man and drink His blood, you have no life in you" (v53). Maybe the truth wasn't what we were looking for after all.

So let's get this straight: the Lamb of God saw large crowds and spoke on things like divorce, hate everything and everybody, and then be a cannibal? That last part might be slightly over-stated, but even the sane derivative to "be consumed with me" was extreme then and now.

The response to his John 6 neighbor day was "many...turned back and no longer followed him" (v66). With only a small crew left afterwards, Jesus did what? Begged them to come back next Sunday? Asked for a hefty contribution so his salary could be made for the week? Nope. He said to them, "Do you want to leave too?" No he did not! Yes He did. Check it out in verse 67. He told them, "There's the door."

Though I'm sure James, John and the faithful few felt like flee-ing, they didn't. Peter acted as spokesman and said something like this: "We'd kind of like to go too. This wasn't our idea of a neighbor-day service. But there is really nowhere to go. We want to go to heaven, and you have the words of eternal life. So I guess we are stuck with each other."

**Fiery Followers**

What did this type of preaching produce? Real, true disciples. Salty salt followers. Committed men and women who turned their world upside down.

The church in the book of Acts was on fire. Christians sold their stuff to help others. Needs were constantly met. These folks met *every day* in the temple courts. The Lord added daily to their number those who were being saved. Many were dying for their faith!

And what do we do? Well, I'm hoping to get my contribution up to 10% some day? Maybe I'll get up the courage to talk to someone about God this week? The first century church was unstoppable. We seem very stoppable. Why? They answered Christ's radical call to committed love, devotion to him that went beyond anyone and anything.

Hebrews 11:35–38 says that average, everyday disciples of God back in the day were sawed in two, stoned, chained and put in prison and more. We very, very rarely have someone call us a "Jesus Freak." Perhaps we miss out on an office party on a weekend or two.

Sometimes I think I am radical because I compare myself to the religious people around me. God's standard is not that. His "normal" is found in the Bible even if that is weird to me. His normal is commitment.

At the end of the day, Christ's call to the masses was that he was looking for salty salt. We want to mix the real stuff with some unsalty grains and have a big pile. We call that "church." Jesus didn't. He actually wanted to separate out that which was unsalty.

Too many of my past neighbor-day Sunday services have been begging people to come back next week, pretty please. I try to convince them how wonderful our kids' classes are and how neat our series will be and how nicely all of our members behave.

Not the man from Nazareth. He threw down. He actually used the word "manure" in a sermon. What he taught was commitment, and what he got from his followers was a commitment that changed the world.

1. What did Jesus preach to large crowds? Why did he do that?

2. What are the most challenging words of Jesus in the Bible to you? How do you react to those words?

3. What difficult things have you gone through because you follow Jesus? Has it been worth it? Why or why not?

# Days 8 & 9
# Character Part 1

## Who Do You Want to Be?

His divine power has given us everything we need for life and godliness through our knowledge of him who called us by his own glory and goodness. Through these he has given us his very great and precious promises, so that through them you may participate in the divine nature and escape the corruption in the world caused by evil desires.

For this very reason, make every effort to add to your faith goodness; and to goodness, knowledge; and to knowledge, self-control; and to self-control, perseverance; and to perseverance, godliness; and to godliness, brotherly kindness; and to brotherly kindness, love.

2 Peter 1:3–7

"Character is like a tree and reputation like a shadow. The shadow is what we think of it; the tree is the real thing."—Abraham Lincoln

What are your goals for this day? This month? This year? Your life? Most people have them. Maybe you want to run a company. Perhaps you want to raise fantastic children. Some want to lose weight, excel academically or help other souls be won to Jesus. All of these are noble ambitions.

What is it you work at the hardest? It is probably these very things you have set as your goals.

The phrase "make every effort" comes up in the New Testament a few times. Here in 2 Peter 1, it is a direct reference to growing in our character. He is not saying "try hard to go on a mission team or get married or become a manager." He is saying our focus, energy, time and heart must be directed at increasing our personal character. How much of your thought and planning goes into that?

## Who God Wants You to Become

Before entering into the character elements mentioned above, 2 Peter 1:5 begins with the words, "For this very reason." Of course, that begs the question, "What very reason?" The preceding verses tell us that because we know God and participate in his divine glory and are called his sons and daughters, we should want to share in his character as well.

It would be really nice if this wasn't a "have to" but a "want to" or an "I get to." For too many of us, Christianity has become a grit-your-teeth-and-bear-it, mega-sacrificial, mindless movement of our bodies to some activities. God wants to fill us with his presence and change everything inside of us for our good and his glory.

I'm going to tell you a little later about my annual staff review I have gone through for many, many years in a few different churches. I think year-end reviews are great, but—to be honest—I don't totally look forward to them. I can easily view them as four or five people telling me my weaknesses. The theory is good, but if they all got ill the day of the review pronouncement, it wouldn't ruin my day.

Our new teen ministry leader just had his first review ever. He walked into the room and said he was so very thrilled to get to go through this exercise. He mentioned that he was so thankful and excited and looked so forward to this time that he had a hard time sleeping the night before.

I didn't like his attitude...because it shamed me so. Here was a man who got it. His review wasn't a "have to" but an "I get to," and it is no wonder his life and ministry are reflecting that before my very eyes.

In this chapter, I don't want to talk about what you ought to do. I want to talk about who you want to be. It is so easy to pursue positions at work, school or church. Are you willing to pursue character with all that you are? That's very different.

You have so much potential. God wants it to blossom from the inside out. There is a sixteen-year-old disciple in our congregation who plays the violin beautifully. What if she just decided to quit today? Everyone who knows her would throw a fit! We'd say, "You are so talented. Don't stop. No matter how hard it is. Keep going. Don't waste the unlimited potential that is so obvious in you!"

I wonder what our Father in heaven thinks about your potential. I know God wants to make beautiful music with your life. You can momo around just doing the basic minimum requirements, I guess. But he wants you to grow and change in increasing ways every day of your life! That's who he created you to be. Will you be that?

## Getting Specific About Character Growth

And then we come to the character areas listed in our theme scripture. The Holy Spirit started with *faith*. Why? Because it is the bedrock of Christianity. It is also what the devil attacks in us most often. You remember prayers that don't seem to have been answered. You look at where your kids are right now in attitude and action. You see relational struggles. All kinds of things kill our belief in God's power in our life (probably he works in others, we think). And Peter cries out with spirit and with the Spirit—don't lose your faith! Start with it and build wherever you are and whatever you are going through.

Character trait #2 is *goodness*. Another translation calls it "moral excellence." We are too satisfied with okayness or moral slightly-above-averageness. That is not the standard of Jesus in speech, conduct or thought. We're comparing ourselves to the wrong person. This is not about the guy who works next to you or the kid in the back of the class throwing spitballs. This is about you going after Christ, who is at the top of the righteousness class.

In Peter's progression, he throws in *knowledge* next. One of the things I love about this list is that it fits everyone. Wherever you are in knowledge—go after learning and applying more. Knowledge is more than facts, but it includes them. If you are a new Christian, memorize the books of the Bible. If you have been around longer, what verses do you have memorized? Can you explain the content of the minor prophets? What would you say to an atheist? You have your whole lifetime to gain and use the insight God gives you. Tomorrow is too late. Go after knowledge in some way today.

And then God gets really serious. He says every person seeking after him should add consistently to their lives *self-control*. I asked a small group in our church last week which of these character issues they most needed to grow in this year. They all answered "self-control" as #1 on their list. This is an interesting one. "Self" tends to take off on us and starts running around wildly. We must learn to increase in "self" control.

Ah yes. Back to my staff review. Each year I am given challenges—delegate more; be more joyful; preach a bit shorter (why do you think we put that big clock on the back wall?). This year, at the very bottom of my report covering about ten subject areas and overall strengths and weaknesses, it said "Eat better and exercise."

Now initially I asked myself, "How do they know I don't eat well and don't exercise?" Then I looked in the mirror. Oh yeah, that's how. Now I have had this chat before with many people. Some say that I need to make sure I am around for the grandkids, and others talk about how much better I will feel. But on this particular day, I asked myself the question, "What would Jesus do?" And the answer I got back was "He'd be in a lot better shape."

And so I decided in this area I really need to practice self-control. I needed to learn some things about calories in and calories out. I needed to say "no" oftentimes to seconds, snacks and Snickers and say "yes" to jogging shoes, prayer walks and Biggest Loser Yoga (my youngest daughter is a beast at this).

What area do you need to practice self-control in? Internet usage? Shopping? Alcohol consumption? Let's go. Make every effort. If the Lord lets me live, I'll have another staff review next year. But over my dead body are they going to say this same thing again!

We're about half way through our character review and I am supposed to stop this chapter. That means this subject is to be continued (I'm somewhat figuring this out on the fly). Your internal progress is to be continued as well. Figure it out too. You can.

1. What are your goals? For the year? For the future?

2. What do you work at the hardest? Why is that?

3. Does your Christianity seem more like a "have to" or a "want to"? How can you be inspired to want it more?

4. How is your faith? Why is it there? How can faith grow in your heart and life?

5. How can you grow in biblical knowledge in the year ahead? Will you take this challenge?

# DAYS 10 & 11
# CHARACTER PART 2

## Nearsighted or 20/20 Vision?

> For if you possess these qualities in increasing measure, they will keep you from being ineffective and unproductive in your knowledge of our Lord Jesus Christ. But if anyone does not have them, he is nearsighted and blind, and has forgotten that he has been cleansed from his past sins.
>
> Therefore, my brothers, be all the more eager to make your calling and election sure. For if you do these things, you will never fall, and you will receive a rich welcome into the eternal kingdom of our Lord and Savior Jesus Christ.
>
> 2 Peter 1:8–11

"Character cannot be developed in ease and quiet. Only through experience of trial and suffering can the soul be strengthened, ambition inspired, and success achieved."—Helen Keller

When I started the preceding chapter, I had no idea it would turn into two. However, character deserves the extra session. No, really it demands it. Let's continue through the Holy Spirit's list of who we are called to be "in increasing measure." We've already looked briefly at faith, goodness, knowledge and self control. If you can believe it—there are more.

**Finishing the Character List**

The next biblical cry to character makes sense right about now because it is God's call to *perseverance*. Other translations say "steadfastness" or "patient endurance." Apparently the Greek word admonishes us to "hold up under the load" graciously.

Do you know what I spend much of my life praying for and trying to make happen? I want the loads to go away. I want to dump the load or get someone else to carry it. That is actually not Christ's plan. He wants us to carry our load with the right spirit.

We all have loads. Yours may be a sick parent. Another person has financial problems. A third has relational conflict with a spouse or a child. Some are in the process of dealing with all of the above and more. In some ways, you have a tougher row to hoe than I do. In other areas I've got you beat. Real Christianity isn't about tossing loads. It is about carrying them graciously.

Let me ask you a very tough question. What if you were told you could pick one of the two following scenarios for the year ahead? Choice A is for life to be smooth sailing—finances fine; healthy; good grades in school or promotion at work, but you don't grow closer to God and maybe even drift from him a bit. Choice B is for life to be very challenging—sickness running rampant; bad grades or loss of job; conflict, but during those twelve months you grow closer to God than you ever have been. Which would you choose? God is more interested in your character than in your comfort.

Next he mentions *godliness*. Whenever I mention the idea of being like God, I get the same response. A united voice comes back, "Well no one is perfect. I can't be like God." Really? I am very grateful for grace, and I know God has, is and will be willing to cover over a multitude of sins. But when did that ever become justification for running away from one of the top goals of our lives: becoming just like Jesus! Get a little faith, and then go after godliness with everything that you are.

Next-to-the-last on this list is *brotherly kindness* or "mutual affection." It is that *phileo* word from which we get our "city of brotherly love," Philadelphia. In the churches I have visited or been a part of, there is generally a feeling of warmth, heart and love in the air. But I think this masks a problem many of us have. We can so easily just become religious. We are acquaintances to many. We can chat about football, the weather and our job. But many of us do not have real brotherly affection. If we did, our conversations and interactions would be much deeper, consistent and life-changing.

Some can't even make it out to any additional services past Sunday. Is that brotherly love? Others don't pick up the phone to call or schedule a time with a brother or sister during the week. Is that what should happen when "family" lives in the same area? Let's not skip this one quickly. Let's show affection as real brothers and sisters who will spend an eternity together.

Finally, Peter closes with *love*. This is *agape*. It is self-sacrificing, unconditional and in-spite-of. It shows up in loving even our enemies. It is Christ on the cross. It is serving. It is living with heart, even if your mate isn't following God (1 Peter 3:1–2). It is turning the other cheek and going the extra mile.

## Make Every Effort

I don't think you would read this book if you didn't want your life to count. You want it to matter. Peter tells us that if we grow in our character, that will keep us from being "ineffective and unproductive." Do you want to have a great family? Work on you. Do you want to have a fantastic church body or campus ministry? Make every effort on your insides.

In these verses, Peter calls us "nearsighted" and "blind." In fact, one translation says, "You are so nearsighted that you are blind." I don't know a lot about many topics, but nearsightedness I understand. I live with that one. I can see fine up close but everything far away is a fog.

This is the human condition and advertisers have a field day. They show you a bedroom set or a flat screen TV and say "No money down for a year!" That is great news for today. But I think we all know that down the road, it can turn into a nightmare as interest overwhelms you and at some point you do have to pay the piper.

The devil is pretty good at this one too. He says, "Take this few minutes on the Internet and enjoy yourself." He doesn't want you to think beyond the moment, to think long-term. He just wants you to drink this or smoke that, to hook up here or chat there. Character is not nearsighted. It is 20/20 vision for this decade on who I want to be for God, family, friends and the next generation.

If you go after God's character in increasing measure, this passage offers a promise: "You will never fall." That is what I want. And then we get a rich welcome (not a "poor" one) into Christ's eternal kingdom. There is no better party I want to attend than that.

Okay, one more time—what do you work hardest at? A dating relationship? The job? Academia? What if it were your character? Pursue that this day. Go after it this week. Live that way this year. And see if this doesn't dramatically change all the rest forever.

## GETTING BACK ON TRACK

1. What loads are on you in life now? How are you doing carrying them?

2. "God is more interested in your character than your comfort." What does this statement mean to you and why?

3. How can you make every effort to grow in the area of brotherly kindness?

4. Who are your enemies or those closest to it? How can you love them?

5. In what ways are you nearsighted spiritually? What would change if you were to have a more long-term 20/20 vision for the future?

# DAYS 12 & 13

# JOY

## Always, Everything and All

I plead with Euodia and I plead with Syntyche to agree with each other in the Lord. Yes, and I ask you, loyal yokefellow, help these women who have contended at my side in the cause of the gospel, along with Clement and the rest of my fellow workers, whose names are in the book of life.

Rejoice in the Lord always. I will say it again: Rejoice! Let your gentleness be evident to all. The Lord is near. Do not be anxious about anything, but in everything, by prayer and petition, with thanksgiving, present your requests to God. And the peace of God, which transcends all understanding, will guard your hearts and your minds in Christ Jesus.

Finally, brothers, whatever is true, whatever is noble, whatever is right, whatever is pure, whatever is lovely, whatever is admirable—if anything is excellent or praiseworthy—think about such things. Whatever you have learned or received or heard from me, or seen in me—put it into practice. And the God of peace will be with you.... I can do everything through him who gives me strength.

Philippians 4:2–9, 13

"Joy is the feeling of grinning inside."
—Melba Colgrove

Rejoice in the Lord. It's a command. It is commanded twice in one short verse. I can only think of one other New Testament passage where God views a law as so important that he repeats it back to back (Galatians 1:8–9). But Paul didn't stop at "rejoice." He said to rejoice in the *Lord*. We aren't told to rejoice in our circumstances or accomplishments. We don't rejoice in our girlfriend or children. This is a God thing. And, as if that were not enough, Paul adds that we are to rejoice *always*. How is that even possible?

Paul often sounds like a super-saint, his lifestyle almost as unattainable as Jesus'. This is one of those times primarily because he is writing this letter from prison! Oh yeah, and prior to that he had been stoned and left for dead, shipwrecked, often without food (2 Corinthians 11:23–28). And he was always happy?

How?

**With Heaven in View**

The answer seems to start with his view of heaven. He got the big picture. He spoke in the passage quoted above about the Book of Life and the Lord being near. He anticipated it. He longed for it. Heaven was really his home, his destination.

From this vantage point, he called out two women in the congregation. Imagine that church service with me. What if your preacher stood up to read a letter from Paul and included your name and the dispute you were having? Wow. That would be a wake-up call. But Paul was saying in essence: Quit fighting! It isn't worth it. One day we will live forever together. Be happy not angry!

I wonder what Paul or Jesus might say in our assemblies? Quit all the marriage squabbling. Stop the gossip. Why all the negativity? And they'd probably name names too. God wants us to look beyond our little world and its meager problems to something way more important.

The author of Philippians says that he wants our gentleness to be evident to all. In the context of relational turmoil, this makes total sense. Another translation says that our reasonableness should be obvious to everyone around us. Can everyone see that you don't hold grudges or that you forgive and resolve matters quickly? Our happiness should be seen and obvious to anyone around us, no matter who has done what or how the day has played out.

It is a sin to not rejoice. I would call you out if I heard you take the name of the Lord in vain. I would say something if I witnessed you robbing a bank. You and I need to speak up about ongoing joylessness in each other's lives. It is not right and is the opposite of the way God intended us to look and live.

## Do Not Be Anxious?

This seems challenging enough, but then God's Spirit adds, "Don't be anxious about anything." Hold on! "Rejoice always" is crazy radical, but we can't worry about *anything* either? Most of us would view this as impossible too. Of course we all worry and stress about some things, right?

Again, the resounding question becomes, "How can any normal person *never* worry?"

The Philippian letter gives us the answer. It is almost too simple: Trust God. We are told to take our requests to him. He can handle them.

I have a friend named Mark. If I gave him $10 and asked him to buy me a sandwich next door while you and I talked, I think he would do it. But what if, as soon as he left, I began to fret about him stealing my $10 and called the police to report a robbery? That would be strange. You would think I don't trust him. But I do trust him and am confident he would fulfill my request. So I wouldn't fret, worry or call the cops.

I wonder how God feels when we say we trust him but then regularly stress about finances, relationships, jobs and more. Our attitude toward him is like he is going to hurt us, steal from us or desert us. Has he ever given us reason to believe that? You worry only when you make a request and don't trust the one of whom you made the request.

## The Peace of God

But if you do trust, the Bible says you can have "the peace of God." We tend to focus on the part that says "which transcends all understanding" and want to figure it out. Listen—if God says you can't understand it, I'd not waste my time trying. But I love just the phrase: "the peace of God."

What kind of peace does God have? Perfect peace. Do you think Jehovah God was all worried in the Old Testament when his people were winning a battle but the sun was about to set and prevent the victory (Joshua 10:1–15)? I don't think so. He can make the sun stand still and he did.

Do you think Jesus was freaking out because he arrived too late to Bethany and Lazarus had already died (John 11:1–44)? To ask it is ridiculous. Raising the dead is just as easy as curing a sickness for Deity. God and Christ had and have complete peace. They can handle the sun, the dead, your bills, any government...and feel free to add anything else to this list.

When you trust you have the peace of God.

## Set Your Mind

This section of God's word closes out by instructing us to set our minds on what is positive—true, noble, right, pure, lovely, admirable, excellent, praiseworthy. We have lots of tapes and videos running through our brains. Some of them are the negative words of parents. Others are pornographic re-runs from years of garbage coming in. There are a lot of angry incidents, unkind words and vengeful feelings rolling through our cranial mush. But we must win the battle of the mind. We must focus on what is excellent and admirable and praiseworthy.

That is why we are instructed to "put it into practice," to think about "such things." These words aren't that new to most of us. Actually following them might be novel and revolutionary.

## Through Him

To close, I want us to remember Philippians 4:13: "I can do everything through him who gives me strength." I am not sure most of us really believe this. I think we believe that we can do *some* things through Christ, and the strong or spiritual might even say we can do *most* things through Christ. This verse says *all* things. In context, this is a reference to being content even if our daily needs are not met. But let's expand it just a bit. What is the *all* for you? Is it quitting smoking? Is it reconciling with your mate? Is it overcoming impurity? Either God is God or he isn't. I think he is. I'm going to go after being happy when it is hard, trusting through the trauma and believing all things in adversity.

Your citizenship is in heaven, no matter what happens with the economy. That is something to rejoice always about.

# GETTING BACK ON TRACK

1. What is it that tends to kill your happiness?

2. What are you looking forward to about heaven?

3. If the apostle Paul were to call you out publicly at a church service, what would it be in reference to?

4. What is your joy level on a scale of 1–10 (10 is the best) and why?

5. The Bible says you can do all things through Christ. What is the one thing at the top of the "all" list which would be the biggest miracle in overcoming? Will you let Jesus help with that?

# MY HEART

# DAY 14
# ALL

## On the Bank or in the River?

But thanks be to God that, though you used to be slaves to sin, you wholeheartedly obeyed the form of teaching to which you were entrusted.

Romans 6:17

"It doesn't take much of a man to be a Christian, but it does take all of him."—Anonymous

If you or I have any hopes of getting back on track with God, we are going to have to give him our all. We must be wholehearted.

Have you ever stood on the banks of a cold river, lake or ocean and watched others have a great time swimming? You have your swimsuit on. You came to swim. You have your goggles and your towel. You want to swim. The only problem is that you stuck your toe in the water and it is freezing out there. You are paralyzed. So you sit and ponder what to do next. At least, you do have options.

First, you can stay on the bank. But watching others have the time of their lives while you are just sitting isn't something you are fond or proud of.

Second, you can just go ahead and dive in. The initial debilitating blast of Arcticness will overtake your body and soul. You will instantly feel miserable. But after a few moments, you know that you will get used to it and then the fun ensues.

Last and definitely least, you can wade in half way. You can inch your way out feeling numbness, getting cranky and ruing the day anyone suggested water sports.

Sadly, most of our world today sits on the not-so-spiritual banks on the wrong side of the Jordan River. Diving in for God seems too radical and extreme. There are too many sacrifices. You have to go against the flow. It can be uncomfortable in Jesus' pond of praying, serving and sharing.

## Take the Plunge

Thankfully, I have been privileged to know many men and women who have taken the big plunge, making Jesus Lord of their lives. No, this wasn't just a baptismal ceremony. It was a death to self and proclamation of giving everything up for the Savior forever more. These disciples' lives are "not their own" (1 Corinthians 6:19). They have gone all in on the Son of God. Their lives are not always easy or comfortable, but they are in the middle of an amazing adventure.

Some of those adventures carry Christ's committed to other nations. Others keep them close to home. However, these im-mersed saints of the Savior have followed in the footsteps of the Old Testament prophets, first-century Christians, martyrs and more in living out the fully devoted life.

The last category is perhaps the scariest to me. It is those who are half in and half out. It is the religious. It is the church at-tendee. It is the God-believing, pot-luck-toting and bumper-sticker-carrying semi-follower of Scripture. It is the man or woman who is so tied to what others think that we talk the same lingo, wear the same clothes, listen to the same music and live pretty close to the same lives as the majority. We just do something different on Sunday mornings, and maybe even another time during the week.

God is clear. Dive in. And for sure, real Christianity is the high dive. It is a bit paralyzing. It takes everything inside of you to jump, and the pool below is not often the comfortable temperature you desire.

## Giving Our All

Mark 12:41–44 tells one of the most amazing stories in all of Scripture. It is familiar—almost too much so. I'm not sure we get it. A poor lady gave two small copper coins, which the Bible is quick to tell us were worth only a fraction of a penny, when the contribution plate was passed around.

Why is that important? I'm kind of appalled that Jesus "sat down opposite the place where people gave their offerings." You shouldn't watch others give, should you? He did. And unashamedly. He was looking for who would give a little, who would give a lot and who would give it *all*. This is more than just a concept tied to money. It is a heart-check and a life exam.

I need to learn more about wholeheartedness. I began a word study of "heart" in just the first few books of the Bible. A quick overview revealed all kinds of negative things my heart can be: hardened (Exodus 7:13), proud (Deuteronomy 8:14), grudging (Deuteronomy 15:10), despairing (Deuteronomy 28:65), wicked (1 Samuel 17:28), terror-filled (1 Samuel 28:5), not fully devoted (1 Kings 11:4), and much more.

Thankfully, my heart can be filled up with good too if I head down that road. My heart can be wise and discerning (1 Kings 3:9), full of integrity (1 Kings 9:4), responsive (2 Kings 22:19), faithful (Nehemiah 9:8), and again, much more.

I must guard my heart (Proverbs 4:23). God can change my heart (1 Samuel 10:9). My heart will be searched (1 Chronicles 28:9) and tested (1 Chronicles 29:17). I have to set my heart (2 Chronicles 19:3). I also need to work with all of my heart for God (Nehemiah 4:6).

Half-heartedness doesn't work in male-female relationships, athletic competition, academia or anything really. It certainly won't cut it with God.

I'm not a good diver. My cannonball is okay. No back flips, for sure. But I'm jumping into the rushing waters of Christianity, and I believe this flow ends in the River of Life (Revelation 22: 1–2), pouring out by the throne of God. There is no greater rapid ride than that.

Where's your heart? Imperfect? That's okay. Tempted? Join the club. All in? It's the only way to dive and it's the only way to thrive with Jesus.

1. What scares you most about diving "all in" to real Christianity?

2. What areas of your life seem half-hearted at best? Why is that?

3. Look at the positive and negative heart aspects mentioned in the brief study of the first few Old Testament books. Evaluate your heart based on these characteristics.

4. What can you do to show God you love him with all you are and have?

# DAY 15

# PASSION

## An Outdoor Service in the Winter

"Love the Lord your God with all your heart and with all your soul and with all your mind and with all your strength. The second is this: 'Love your neighbor as yourself.' There is no commandment greater than these."

Mark 12:30

"Those who danced were thought to be quite insane by those who could not hear the music."

—Angela Monet

Life is boring without passion. The driving force behind great art, music, drama and architecture is passion. It seems you can be passionate about anything and everything, except God.

If you type "book" and "a passion for" into your Internet search engine, you will come up with over twelve million hits. There are titles of books for all things imaginable, and some you would never imagine. All of the following are titles starting with "A Passion for": Radio, Pineapples, Chocolate [understandable], Mushrooms, Birds, Potatoes, Tarpon [a type of fish—the price of the book is $100], Needlepoint, Cactus, and Steam. Can you really be infatuated with steam?

### Showing Passion for God

On our coldest Connecticut day in January, I suggested to our congregation that we have an outdoor service at the park down the street. They recoiled in horror. "What about our children?" someone queried, in a tone of voice that implied their kids were not foremost in their minds.

In a quick effort to save my job, I told the crowd we would not be meeting outside that day. It was all a joke. However, I did inform them that two professional football games would be played that same day. Both locations of NFL cities were forecast to have snow, freezing rain, gusty winds and sub-zero wind-chill factors. Both football stadiums hold over 60,000 fans and would be filled to beyond capacity. In addition to this, each attendee would pay hundreds of dollars for the privilege of being outside to see these once-in-a-lifetime play-off games.

As I said, you can be passionate about everything but God in today's world. Here, you have to sit quietly at a church service. It works best if you have a long, sad face and hands folded on your lap. You get bonus points if you throw a dollar or two into the collection plate, but that is not required.

If you get passionate about Jesus, you are considered a cult member at worst and a Bible Banger at best.

In the middle of this mentality, I opened my Bible and read the greatest commandment. It says (in The Message translation) to "love the Lord your God with all your passion and prayer and intelligence and energy."

The #1 thing it seems our Father is searching for is a love filled with every bit of passion inside us. And that should start with a love for him. In the first century, people traveled long distances on foot to hear Christ. Do you consistently drive a few minutes to fellowship, attend Bible studies and learn from his word? Back in the day, hundreds died for him. Are you willing to live for him now?

## Passion for God's People

But beyond God himself, we must have a passion for his people, his church. My guess is that most of you reading this know that "church" is not a building or a service time. Real church is about living in a community of people who have Jesus as their common focus. This authentic community is not about where you go but how you live.

In Acts 2, we are told that the original disciples took care of every need of the fellow members of Christ's body, met daily in the temple courts, and grew in number and faith.

Virtually no one I know can understand why someone from the Deep South would move and spend a lifetime in cold New England (including myself sometimes). The answer is simple. It is not about the piles of snow but the partners. It isn't the barometric pressure that is most important but the brothers and sisters. I'm the happiest I have ever been in my igloo, I mean, house.

The Acts story is a picture of a passionate—not perfect—church. It was really unstoppable. Today, most churches are very stoppable. Just sprinkle in some rain and many are scared off. Have a favorite song leader move away, and watch the people run somewhere else for entertainment. Don't you dare have a kids' class craft be below average or Mom and Dad may be gone by the next service.

Where are the men and women with a heart-felt passion for God and people? Where are the warriors that are sticking with Christ and his plan first no matter what comes or who goes?

## Saying 'I Do' to God

I said "I do" to Anita over twenty-five years ago and she alone is the one I chase (okay, and annoy sometimes too). I am passionate toward her today because she has remained the object of my focus, intention and desire. It helps that she is cute and sweet, but that is a fringe benefit. I'm looking for and finding all kinds of reasons to love and be enamored with her and her alone.

Most of us have also said "I do" to pursue a relationship with God for the long haul. I know I annoy God a lot. If honest, I have to say that he annoys me too on some occasions. I became a part of a spiritual family—with some cool and some fairly weird brothers and sisters (if the shoe fits, wear it). My passion in life and yours is to be focused on two things primarily: not money, not my kids' sports, not my career, nothing else but a passion for God and people.

## GETTING BACK ON TRACK

1. What things are you most passionate about? Why?

2. How can you show your passion for God?

3. How can you show your passion for God's people?

4. In what ways do the marriage vows parallel our commitment to God and his church?

5. How can you keep passion burning for the long haul spiritually? Ask some other close friends how they do it. Will you persevere?

# Days 16 & 17
# SPIRIT

## Something That Goes Beyond Christmas

But it is the spirit in a man, the breath of the Almighty,
that gives him understanding.

Job 32:8

The lamp of the LORD searches the spirit of a man;
it searches out his inmost being.

Proverbs 20:27

"The spirit, the will to win, and the will to excel
are the things that endure. These qualities are
so much more important than the events that
occur."—Vince Lombardi

World War I was raging in 1914. On the bitterly cold battle-
fields of the Western Front thousands of soldiers were dying. On
one small battlefield in Belgium, an event took place that may
never be repeated again. A few different stories are told of these
events. Though some of the small stuff may be slightly off, the
big thing is what you have to get.

On Christmas Eve, 1914, the British fighters were lying low
in their trenches. On the other side of No Man's Land, the
Germans kept their heads down in trenches too. But it was
Christmas Eve, so a few Brits somehow put up some lights in
a couple of trees. At first, the Germans were suspicious that
new weaponry was being brought in. Later, though, they under-

stood. One German started singing, "Stille Nacht" (which, being interpreted, is "Silent Night") and was joined by others. The Englishmen applauded. Then the British sang and the Germans clapped.

After some awkward silence, one soldier rose from his side of the battlefield and walked into the middle of No Man's Land. Before long an adversary from the other side walked into the forbidden zone too. After a while, several soldiers gathered in the middle of the two armies and began to exchange items: cigarettes, pudding, clothing, etc.

The next day, December 25, the truce continued. A soccer match was played (rumor has it that the Germans won 3–2). Several bodies of fallen, frozen warriors were given a proper burial. Someone even read the twenty-third Psalm. A few from the two sides swapped names and addresses for contact after the war, if they were to make it out alive.

The story is told that one side held up a sign saying, "Merry Christmas," at the end of the day, and the enemy retorted with their own homemade message, "Thank You." The sun went down on Christmas day.

On the morning of December 26, 1914, the killing commenced. The war was to last another four years, and about nine million people were killed in all. Many wonder if Europe to this day has fully recovered from the massacre and bloodshed. Upon hearing of this two-day stoppage, the report came down from the commanding officers that this type of mini-peace must never happen again. To my knowledge, it hasn't.

I have seen pictures taken in what was then No Man's Land in the area of Ypres, Belgium. They depict a cross which stands even now remembering the long-past truce with the words, "Khaki Chums Christmas Truce—Lest We Forget."

There is something very special about the end of December. We call it the spirit of Christmas. People seem to thaw a bit on the inside. Even in cold New England where I live, some occasionally say "Hello" and "How are you?" at this time of year.

Thanksgiving is special too. Food, fun, family and football seem to take over many households. We think of those we love and maybe of those we have loved and lost too.

I am reminded of September 11, 2001. It was a tragic day for all US citizens. But the aftermath of those vivid events brought intense acts of love, service, sacrifice and heart. People actually seemed to care again...for a little while.

But then we went back to real life. We got selfish again. We started looking out for #1.

The Christmas spirit is great, but it typically ends on December 26. Life's busyness—work, the rat race, school starting back up, trading in unwanted gifts and more—takes control of us again. A long time ago Elvis Presley sang a song with these lyrics: "Why can't every day be like Christmas?"

Perhaps it is because we don't just need the spirit of Christmas; we need the spirit of Christ. We don't just need a season; we need a Savior. We can't just celebrate Thanksgiving with turkey in November; we must give thanks continually (1 Thessalonians 5:18).

## The Holy Spirit Inside

There are many lessons here. One is everyone's need for the Holy Spirit to live inside us. This too often forgotten part of the Deity was left behind by Jesus because he is essential to our ongoing spirituality. The Comforter, as he is called, strengthens us (Ephesians 3:16), guides us into all truth (John 16:13), intercedes in our prayers (Romans 8:26), produces godly fruit in our lives (Galatians 5:22–23), and the like.

But we also need a stronger, consistent spirit. Spirit in this context means attitude. Too many of us are moody. Too many of us are hot and cold for God and his will. We get fired up on Sunday but fade away the next six days. We want to pray or sing or speak publicly when our congregation meets, but we lose heart privately the next hour.

Life for God is not a sprint. It is a marathon. Some experience "runner's high" (I'm still waiting for that to happen, so I can't comment). Most of us will put one foot in front of the other mile after mile with a tenacious spirit in order to persevere to the end.

Author and speaker Stuart Briscoe said something like this:

> The spirit of Christmas needs to be superseded by the Spirit of Christ. The spirit of Christmas is annual; the Spirit of Christ is eternal. The spirit of Christmas is sentimental; the Spirit of Christ is supernatural. The spirit of Christmas is a human product. The Spirit of Christ is a divine person.

Is God's spirit in you? What kind of spirit or attitude do you have? I'm a part of a fellowship that enjoys the radical part of Jesus and first-century Christianity, and I am grateful for that. Jesus fasted forty days. First-century Christians added to their number daily. The gospel spread when disciples were being regularly killed on crosses afire and as they were thrown to lions.

But I think consistent is radical too. I have seen many largely unknown men and women who love God and spend time with him every day. I know uneducated followers of our Master who open their mouths and speak up at virtually every opportunity. I see some who memorize Scripture, serve the poor and give their sacrificial contribution week after week because they signed up to be married to Jesus for better or for worse.

These heroes don't just dress up on Christmas. Their spirit is touched by God's Holy Spirit, and that Spirit is daily changing them. Let it change you too.

## GETTING BACK ON TRACK

1. How would you describe your spirit when going through difficult circumstances?

2. What are the greatest blessings to you from the Holy Spirit?

3. Are you moody? If so, how does that show up in your daily life?

4. How can you grow in controlling your emotional fluctuations to be more like Christ?

# DAYS 18 & 19
# DESPERATE

## Why Stay Here Until We Die?

Now there were four men with leprosy at the entrance
of the city gate. They said to each other, "Why stay
here until we die? If we say, 'We'll go into the city'—
the famine is there, and we will die. And if we stay
here, we will die. So let's go over to the camp of the
Arameans and surrender. If they spare us, we live; if
they kill us, then we die."

2 Kings 7:3–4

"For a desperate disease a desperate cure."
—Michel de Montaigne

"Desperate times call for desperate measures."
—Anonymous

The devil is good at what he does. He doesn't usually move us
from disciple to atheist overnight. He likes to put us to spiritual sleep while our lives drift closer and closer to the perilous
waterfall. Perhaps you are thinking…"It seemed like at one
point God and I were best friends, but now he is so far away.
How did I get here? How did this happen?"

I'm not sure I can explain all the reasons. However, I do know
that scary times away from God are cause for the greatest alarm
in your life. I know people who have cancer, Alzheimer's and
multiple sclerosis. I am very sympathetic to those with these ill-

nesses. But I don't think any of these compare to the destructive plight of distance or separation from Jesus.

I think if you are further from God today than you were last year, last month or last night—it is time to get alarmed. There can be a great benefit to righteous desperation.

In 2 Kings 7, the story is told of four lepers. But first, let's set the stage. Ben-Hadad, king of Aram, and his army had laid siege to Samaria. A great famine struck the land since he cut off all food supplies. People were eating their children (2 Kings 6:28–29), donkeys' heads and more.

The king of Israel had no idea what to do. He correctly surmised, "This disaster is from the Lord" (2 Kings 6:33). However, he decided to kill Elisha the prophet, in the spirit of "if you can't stop the message just shoot the messenger." But if God doesn't want his prophet dead, it isn't going to happen. So Elisha lived on and prophesied that the problem with the Arameans would be over within twenty-four hours. The king's officer scoffed at this idea and would die for his faithlessness later in the chapter.

So that brings us back to these four sick men who, by the way, were going to die from their incurable disease at some point in the not-too-distant-future anyway. The lepers asked a question we should all ask more often, "Why stay here until we die?" There are many ways to pass away physically and spiritually. Sitting around isn't the best way to go out in a blaze of glory.

There are a lot of lessons to learn from this amazing story. One is that we should believe God's word. If he says through his prophet that the problem will be solved soon, I'd nod in agreement. If his word says that he will not forsake the righteous (Psalm 37:25), it is true. If he says that a person's soul will be demanded 100% of the time for greed ("this is how it will be with anyone who stores up things for himself but is not rich toward God" in Luke 12:21), I'd shudder.

## Do Something

But here is the main point I want you to get about *you* today. God will be God, and I'm not so concerned about him. I want to call *you* to do *something!* That is what desperate people who want to get out of their messes do. They do something! It can't be "nothing." You can't just sit around and get out of your problems or spiritual funk.

In the case of the lepers, they outrageously walked into the enemy's army camp. Certain death would seem to await them. First, they were Israelites. Next, they were lepers. These were not the type of people the Arameans would want around. But it ended up being the Arameans who weren't around!

Not only is God's word true, but God is all powerful. He had caused his people's enemies to hear noises in the dusk and get paranoid. They left everything behind and ran for their lives. Amazing! Not only were the lepers safe, but now they were well fed, well clothed and well off in every way imaginable.

That's how God dealt with their desperation. How will he deal with yours?

It depends. Will you do something? Will you start back down the long and winding prodigal son road? Will you pray? I'm not talking about for an hour a day. I'm asking you to share a few sentences that are real and from the heart. Get going. Will you humble out and call someone who might be able to help? Will you stop hanging with the "bad company" (1 Corinthians 15:33)? Will you go serve someone poor today? Someone who is much worse off than yourself to help end the pity party you've been throwing?

I think it is interesting that in many of Jesus' greatest healing miracles he asks the sick to do something, even though it is very small. Check these out: "Rise up and walk." "Go show yourself to the priest." "Go wash in the pool of Siloam." Christ could have had the lame man float into the air. But he didn't. He wanted the man to do something. He calls you and me to the same.

## Share the Wealth

But the story doesn't end there. For the stirring conclusion, the lepers also came to their senses the way many of us need to come to ours today. They realized how much they had been blessed by this miracle and said, "We can't keep this under wraps." Their exact words were, "We're not doing right. This is a day of good news and we are keeping it to ourselves" (2 Kings 7:9).

So the four lepers spread the news to all of Israel. Though the king and others didn't believe them at first, they were eventually persuaded. And in twenty-four hours, God's people had all they needed to eat, wear and live for again.

Part of our being close to God is sharing what we have—the greatest news ever—with others around us. We can't keep it to ourselves. Have you stopped doing that? Maybe they will believe you. Maybe not. It doesn't matter. Maybe people were interested when I got engaged to Anita many years ago. Maybe not. I didn't care. I told them anyway.

Recently an old white man came to visit one of our morning church services. I asked him why he had come. He said he met a young African American man in the mall, and he had to come and see what that youngster was so fired up about. He didn't remember his name. He didn't remember anything specific about the conversation. He just knew this young man was on fire, and he wanted to see what caused the sparks.

Are you desperate today? I hope so. Channel that "panic under control" to inspire you to move for and with God today and all the days of your life. Then tell somebody else to come along and join you.

## GETTING BACK ON TRACK

1. What are you most desperate about now and why?

2. Do you believe God can change circumstances? Why or why not?

3. Are you an active or passive person? How do you think Jesus lived his life and how can you be more like him?

4. What action encourages you the most spiritually? Why?

5. How have you been doing recently in sharing your faith?

6. What is the good news God has given you to share?

# DAY 20
# RELENTLESS

## Thoughts for Crumb Lovers

Leaving that place, Jesus withdrew to the region of Tyre and Sidon. A Canaanite woman from that vicinity came to him, crying out, "Lord, Son of David, have mercy on me! My daughter is demon-possessed and suffering terribly." Jesus did not answer a word. So his disciples came to him and urged him, "Send her away, for she keeps crying out after us."

He answered, "I was sent only to the lost sheep of Israel."

The woman came and knelt before him. "Lord, help me!" she said.

He replied, "It is not right to take the children's bread and toss it to the dogs."

"Yes it is, Lord," she said. "Even the dogs eat the crumbs that fall from their master's table."

Then Jesus said to her, "Woman, you have great faith! Your request is granted." And her daughter was healed at that moment.

Matthew 15:21–28


"Nature is relentless and unchangeable, and it is indifferent as to whether its hidden reasons and actions are understandable to man or not."

—Galileo Galilei


What would you like for God to say to you right now? "Well done good and faithful servant"? "Here, have a husband or wife"? "The raise is coming"? What would you wish for? How about this sentence: "You have great faith and whatever you request is granted"? I'd be up for that.

The Bible tells a story that ends this way. However, most of us miss the ending and don't even like the story because of the beginning and middle part of the tale.

Jesus, it would seem, spent 99% of his life in Israel. Very rarely did he venture out. But in the Matthew 15 text above (and Mark 7), Jesus left his home turf and talked with a Canaanite woman. Well, actually, the woman initiated the conversation by crying out to him. The Bible says she was requesting help for her daughter who was "suffering terribly."

There is something special about a mother's compassion for her kids. I am not the most emotionally connected individual around, but even I get misty-eyed seeing the heartache of a mom hurting for her child. I've seen some mothers wailing and sobbing and inconsolable. Jesus didn't seem to clue in to her desperation. God's word says, "[He] did not answer a word." Not a word?

What do you do when God is silent? Have you ever felt like that? To ask it is to answer it. We all have. We want a child… nothing. We want to be effective with the lost…zero. We'd just like a date occasionally…crickets.

You know what most people do? They quit. They give up on the whole God thing. It probably seemed rude to the Canaanite lady, and it seems downright disrespectful to us. The Lamb of God said nothing. But this little-known female responded with persistent, relentless faith.

**Scene Two**

Enter to what we'll call scene two—the sensitive apostles of our Lord. Their first comment in unison is, "Send her away." Okay, maybe the silence was better.

What do you do when God's people hurt you? Has that ever happened to you? An unkind comment? An event you weren't invited to? Harshness? Of course, it is not "has it happened," but "how often," right?

You know what many people do with hurtful words and deeds from fellow Christians? They use it as an excuse to drop Jesus, Christianity and the Scriptures. They begin to throw the "hypocrite" word around, and maybe even justifiably so. But our female outsider responded with persistent, relentless faith.

**Scene Three**

As the story-line heads to its climactic end, our Savior finally speaks. We'll call it scene three. We love the Shepherd's words of comfort. We delight in his heart and even tears for people found in God's Holy Book. Here is pretty much what he said this time, "I can't take Israel's bread and throw it to you Gentile dogs."

What do you do when Jesus' words seem too strong and overwhelming? A great number of people read no further and stash their Bible away never to be seen or heard from again.

Virtually all the commentaries I have ever read regarding this story tell me that there are two different kinds of dogs that ran in Palestine. There were the rabid, scary dogs and there were the calmer, pet-type. The type referred to here, they emphasize, is the family pet. This is supposed to make me feel better about Christ's words? Sorry, from any angle, our Lord just called her a dog (pit bull or Chihuahua, take your pick).

Did you realize that Christ commanded several other challenging things during his life on earth? He said, "Hate your father and mother." "Forgive 70 × 7." "Take up your cross daily." In principle he challenged us all to stay true to our marriage vows no matter what, to run away from lust, to give sacrificially and cheerfully, to fast and pray, and much more.

What do we learn from this un-named Gentile? Persistent, re-lentless faith. She actually said to the Messiah, "Even dogs get the crumbs." Being interpreted, she said, "Can you give my daughter (not even 'me') just a little something?" And Jesus finally did.

## Life Tests Us

In lots of ways, life is a test. I want life to be all about celebration. Nope. Too bad. That's heaven. I don't like tests of any sort. I like victories, successes, baptisms and thanksgiving sharing sessions. Okay, that is duly noted, but God and the devil both give out a few exams. And the Canaanite woman passed with flying colors.

So the King of Kings and Lord of Lords proclaimed, "You have great faith! Your request is granted." I love the ending. I'm not always so enthralled with the other part. But you don't get the cool phrase until you pass the test.

Your life can end with this amazing declaration from God. But you don't get to say how it all goes down right now. Where's the husband? Why the foreclosure? Why no father in my life? Why this disease? How come it is so hard? I don't know. Only God does, and he's not necessarily explaining everything right now.

Christ constantly tested his disciples: "You give them some-thing to eat." "You cast out the demons." "Go out two by two without bags packed or money on you."

Perhaps, like a Canaanite or a canine, we should be less de-manding of God. Maybe we should humble out and realize we are not entitled to it our way.

Wouldn't it be something if we just focused on persistent, re-lentless faith and then hung in there long enough—maybe even to the end—to get the blessing?

## GETTING BACK ON TRACK

1. What does the word "relentless" mean to you?

2. Think of a time in your life when you felt like God was silent. How did you handle his silence?

3. Think of a time when you were hurt by another Christian.
   How did you handle that pain?

4. What are some things in God's word that seem too strong or
   demanding for you? How do you deal with those passages?

5. How is God testing you now?

6. How can you grow in your faith and pass the ultimate eternal test?

# MY HANDS

# DAYS 21 & 22

# GIVE

## Sell Everything

"Two things I ask of you, O LORD;
   do not refuse me before I die.
Keep falsehood and lies far from me;
give me neither poverty nor riches,
   but give me only my daily bread.
Otherwise, I may have too much
and disown you and say, 'Who is the LORD?'
Or I may become poor and steal,
   and so dishonor the name of my God."
                                            Proverbs 30:7–9

"We make a living by what we get, but we make a life by what we give."—Winston Churchill

We have an annual special-missions contribution in our church. This year, we decided to do it differently. We swapped wallets and purses...and then we gave for each other.

Okay, we didn't actually go through with it. We did do the swap and then thought about it, before I chickened out. I decided I needed my job. And, you know, as I held my friend's wallet, I was extremely ready to give. I knew he had plenty. Both he and his wife work. They have no kids. They live in a less expensive part of town. As opposed to my wallet, there was real money sitting right inside his. If I would have given for him, I would have given a lot...and super joyfully!

But then I got my wallet back. My wife only works part time. The four girls in my household spend full-time. Of my three daughters, two are in college (out-of-state tuition, I might add). Heating costs in New England are through the roof. Health care, gasoline, phone bills and mortgage payments are hitting me hard in tough economic times. I love God and would like to give more, but everyone should understand that life is difficult and I can't. That's what my wallet told me.

At this same church service, I asked, "How many of you are rich, middle class or poor?" Of the approximate 450 people in attendance that day three people raised their hands as "rich." The overwhelming majority responded to "middle class" and several admitted they were "poor."

I read a few statistics. You've probably heard these type numbers before: 53% of the world's population lives on less than $2.50 a day. One billion people (out of 6.8 billion in the world) live on less than $1 a day. I am now looking at a report of the countries with massive percentages of people earning under $2 a day. It is startling: Nigeria at 90.8%; Mali at 90.6%; Zambia at 87.4%; India at 86.2%; etc. The list is long and exhausting. Basically insert here that all African nations are in extreme poverty. The Middle East is struggling mightily. Many Spanish speaking nations have large segments of their people in deep distress. The needs for basic food, clothing and medicines are overwhelming.

Guess what? We in the USA are rich. We are not middle class. We don't even begin to "get" poverty. You are rich. I am rich. We are all very wealthy. But there is a larger point I want to make. This isn't about feeling guilty. This is about how you and I read the Bible.

I decided I was going to read God's Word like I was a rich person for the first time ever. I have mostly read his stories with a middle class view. Back in the day, as a child in Arkansas, I even read from a "poor" perspective because my state finished 49th in everything: per capita income, education, millionaires, etc. (I thanked the Good Lord many times for Mississippi, #50.)

I read again the story of the rich man and Lazarus. I have always viewed Donald Trump and friends as the people with no compassion walking by the one in need. Donald Trump doesn't even live near a place where you would find a poor man. That story is not about him. It is about me and my lack of heart.

I read too about the rich young ruler. He was very religious, majored in morality and knew lots of facts about the Ten Commandments. That is not a picture of Bill Gates. That is a bullseye, dead-on snapshot of me.

And then Jesus said something totally crazy to me, the rich not-so-young preacher. Right there in his inerrant Word. He said, "Give it *all* away."

I have a lifetime to give everything away. And this does include money. But it goes beyond money too. You and I must give away all that we know to younger Christians, to the lost, to the next generation and everyone we see. We must give away our talents. Can you sing or play? Can you preach or build? Can you write or clean or draw? Can you relate with a prisoner? Can you love someone who is homeless? Can you carry things from your garage down to the mission's tag sale? Give everything you have got away.

The Bible's widow with two mites got it right. The widow from Zarephath who shared with Elijah her last remaining cake of bread was on target (I've never called bread "cake" before, but if it was all I had, I probably would). Rich people don't figure this out very often, and that is why it is very hard for them—check that—for *us* to make it to heaven (have you ever noticed how "us" spells us and also US?).

Did you read that opening prayer in Proverbs 30? That was written by an Old Testament unknown, Agur, son of Jakeh. Jakeh could have probably come up with a better name for his off-spring, but he sure produced an amazing child.

Agur said, "Don't give me poverty!" Oh, I have prayed that one before and heard many scream it from the mountaintops in assorted ways. Then he added, "Don't give me riches because they might cause me to be self-reliant and disown my Lord." That I have never prayed. I have never ever heard anyone pray it. Not even close.

Let's start praying Agur's prayer. I know the prayer of Jabez sounds better: "Enlarge my territory" (1 Chronicles 4:9–10)! But the prayer of the righteous, rich man is sometimes a bit different: "Give me the strength, O Father. Whatever I've got or get, I'm giving away till the day I die."

Do you want to please God, really? Do you want to follow him no matter what? Then start today and give it all away. I'm not sure how much longer we're going to live...so we rich folks had better get started.

1. How would you feel about giving financially if you were the richest member of your congregation? Is that the way you feel now? Why or why not?

2. Are you rich, middle class or poor? In light of that answer, what is the Bible teaching you about giving?

3. What do you personally have to give away until the day you die? What is your plan to go about doing that?

4. Compare and contrast the prayers of Agur and Jabez.

# DAYS 23 & 24
# DIE

## Don't Forget to Scrub Between the Toes

"You call me 'Teacher' and 'Lord,' and rightly so, for that is what I am. Now that I, your Lord and Teacher have washed your feet, you also should wash one another's feet. I have set you an example that you should do as I have done for you. I tell you the truth, no servant is greater than his master, nor is a messenger greater than the one who sent him. Now that you know these things, you will be blessed if you do them."

John 13:13–17

"Death may be the greatest of all human blessings."—Socrates

I died today…in a sense. Oh, I'm still breathing and all. But trust me—this feels like death.

For the past several years, I have lived at twenty-five to thirty pounds above where I should be. When young, I participated in a sport every season. I could eat anything and everything (and I did) because I was easily sweating off the calories in the scorching Arkansas sun at football practice, shooting hoops, and playing tennis and other sports.

But now, my schedule tends to revolve around the best times to get with people. Those are breakfast, lunch, dinner and late-night snacks. As I write this chapter in the frozen winter of

New England, I realize the height of my caloric burn is often the fifteen yards walking from my front door to the warming car outside.

So I have a friend—who today feels like an enemy; but trust me, he is my friend—who sent me to a Web site. At that site, you enter how many pounds you want to lose a week. In order to do that, it tells you how many calories you can eat per day. You log in everything you eat and it tells you the truth.

So, for my initial meal, I had a salad. I actually don't mind salads. But for the first time ever, I had nonfat ranch dressing on top. I honestly think kerosene would have tasted better. It was really nasty. The water with no lemon was the highlight of my meal.

Now, I have done many radical things before in dealing with pounds. I have fasted for a long time. I have given up desserts. I have stopped drinking soda. Exercise commitments rise and fall. But this was an overall lifestyle change for the long haul. Well, we'll see how long the haul is. I survived day one.

## Dying 101

What does it mean to die? We'd better figure that one out because Jesus said, "I tell you the truth, unless a kernel of wheat falls to the ground and dies, it remains only a single seed. But if it dies, it produces many seeds" (John 12:24). Christianity is a call to die. But in that death comes life for you and others, Christ said in the next verse (John 12:25).

Jesus made this puzzling statement at the end of John 12, and I'm sure the apostles were scratching their heads wondering what he was talking about. Then he showed them.

What if you had your ten or twelve best friends over for a big meal—let's say a pizza party? Woops, scratch that...let's say a grapes and strawberries hangout (can't kill all your calories for the week in one shot). Maybe you are watching the Super Bowl or playing a board game (ladies—just a side point, pet peeve— quit always suggesting the teams be divided men against the women for *Pictionary*. Please; I beg you). In the middle of the chaos, loud music and small-scale food fight, what if your third-best buddy, Freddie, got up and started taking everyone's shoes off? Then, what if he went for the socks too?

I mean, everyone would definitely think Freddie was weird. There would be some sarcastic comments about the room odor. Probably someone would pipe up about toe fungus. But after a few minutes, I'm pretty sure the room would get very quiet.

And what if Freddie then brought in a pail of water, some soap and a rag and started cleaning feet? Awkward. And what if he went around the entire room? That would mean he even washed Melanie's feet—the girl who broke up with him because Johnny was cuter. He would have washed Nate's feet—who plays first string quarterback and keeps Freddie riding the bench behind him. And then what if he came to you? Now this was your party and Freddie is certainly blowing the vibe....

## Jesus the Teacher

In John 13, the divine Son of God stooped down at a meal with his best friends and washed a lot of dirty feet. No one expected it. No one enjoyed it. I'm guessing things got quiet for a while. He washed Judas' feet. Judas had turned traitor. He had stolen money from Jesus and his friends. He was about to hand the Savior of the world over to be killed. I talk to many married couples who excuse their horrific behavior because their spouse did something mean first. In the face of cruelty and deceit, Jesus removed sandals and scrubbed.

Christ washed the feet of a tax collector who had helped the Romans. He cleaned in between the toes of a Zealot who hated the

Romans. And then he came to Simon Peter with his bucket and towel. This was a very uncomfortable moment. So this impetuous follower said what others had thought, "You shall never wash my feet." If I had been brave enough to speak (doubtful), that's what I would have said too.

Jesus, who seems to me was always trying to run his followers off versus begging them to stay, then said, "Unless I wash you, you have no part with me." In my top ten statements by human beings in the whole Bible, Peter replied, "Then not just my feet but my hands and my head as well." In plain English, he was saying that Jesus could just go ahead and give him a bath.

## The Call to Die

You know the rest of the story. Jesus told his guys that he washed feet to give them an example for how they should treat others. They would need to spend a lifetime serving when they didn't feel like it, on their knees on the floor when they would have preferred the sofa, and dying when the world around them was living it up.

Jesus wasn't calling anyone to a life of Sunday temple attendance for two hours. He was shouting loudly and clearly through his life that every day, every true follower of his was going to be doing a whole lot of stooping, serving...and dying.

Here's the kicker—they got the message. They *went* into all the world, when it would have been much easier to *stay*. They had watched their Master heal and help many, and now they went out to touch lepers, lift up the crippled and feed the hungry. They had witnessed their mentor die a torturous death while being completely innocent.

And now they would go and die.

Check out this one listing of what Adrian Dieleman's research says happened to some first-century followers.[1]

*Matthew suffered martyrdom by being slain with the sword in Ethiopia.*

*Mark perished at Alexandria, after being cruelly dragged through the streets of that city.*

*Luke was hanged upon an olive tree in Greece.*

*John was put in a pot of boiling oil, but escaped death. He was later branded and then exiled in Patmos.*

*Peter was crucified at Rome with his head downward (unworthy to die like Jesus, he said).*

*James, the brother of John, was beheaded in Jerusalem.*

*James, the son of Alphaeus, was thrown from a lofty point of the temple and then beaten to death with a club.*

*Bartholomew was whipped to death.*

*Andrew was bound to a cross, from which he preached to his persecutors until he died.*

*Thomas was run through the body with a lance in the East Indies.*

*Jude was shot to death with arrows.*

*Matthias was first stoned and then beheaded.*

*Barnabas was stoned to death at Salonica.*

*Paul, after many tortures and persecutions, was beheaded in Rome by Nero.*

---

[1]From a sermon preached on May 3, 1998, at Trinity United Reformed Church in Visalia, CA.

## Our Response?

I need to not eat so much and exercise more. What? I need to follow Jesus more. I need to quickly turn off the TV and make some phone calls to others who are struggling. I must go out into the cold and drive my car over to counsel a troubled brother or sister. I have no choice but to sacrifice my money so that people in other places can hear about the best news there has ever been.

It is way past time for me to serve, to give, to love, to sacrifice, to clean feet, to touch the diseased, to open my mouth. It is time for me to die. And maybe in more ways than one.

GETTING BACK ON TRACK

1. What is the #1 thing you know you currently need to die to?

2. Who has served you in the most inspiring ways in the past? How? How did that feel?

3. Do you believe you would be willing to be tortured or even killed for Jesus today? Why or why not?

4. Who can you serve this month? How? When?

# DAY 25

# DIG

## Only God Can Send the Stream, but You Can Grab a Shovel

"This is what the LORD says, Make this valley full of ditches. For this is what the LORD says, You will see neither wind nor rain, yet this valley will be filled with water and you, your cattle and your other animals will drink. This is an easy thing in the eyes of the LORD; he will also hand Moab over to you. You will overthrow every fortified city and every major town. You will cut down every good tree, stop up all the springs, and ruin every good field with stones."

The next morning, about the time for offering sacrifice, there it was—water flowing from the direction of Edom! And the land was filled with water.

2 Kings 3:16–20

"Sitting still and wishing made no person great. The good Lord sends the fish, but you must dig the bait."—Anonymous

It is appropriate that in 2 Kings 3, three kings were coming to Elisha looking for water. Their armies were parched, their animals fatigued. Defeat seemed inevitable as these three kings prepared to fight against the powerful army of Moab. Only in desperation did they cry out, "Is there no prophet of the Lord we may inquire of?"

Ultimately they settled on Elisha. They had no idea what they were getting themselves into. One of the things I love about God's prophets past or present is that they speak clearly and you don't walk away wondering what they meant. Elisha was not a big fan of the covenant between God's people and other kings during this warring venture. His first comment was, "If I did not have respect for the presence of Jehoshaphat, king of Judah, I would not look at you or even notice you" (v14). My, that was endearing.

But then Elisha called for a musician—the NIV says "a harpist." Too many folks go through life upset and they just need to find some music to listen to. It is interesting how the Old Testament heroes played music to soothe, inspire and help change people or moods. But I digress...

At the end of 2 Kings 3, God's prophet said, "Dig ditches!" It was an interesting command. My first question, had I been present that day, would have been, "Why?" Digging ditches is long, hard and thankless work. It is not something anyone should do for no reason.

I would assume the kings looked skyward and saw no clouds. What were they to do? What would you do? They dug. Their people dug. What other choice did they have? The prophet of God had spoken.

As you know, the next day water came. And it came. And it came. The ditches were filled. All drank deeply and the kings went on to victory over Moab. It's a nice obscure story hidden away in 2 Kings.

**Waiting for Water**

I see a lot of people sitting around and waiting for "water" to come into their lives. They want success. They desire a great family. They're looking for a better job. Perhaps they want to get back close to God again or have a life of high impact on others. But there is nothing they see on the horizon and not a cloud in the sky.

Please get this principle today: Only God can send a stream, but you can dig a ditch. I've heard it said before that you do the natural and God will do the supernatural. You must dig today for tomorrow's $H_2O$.

In the spirit of honesty, I must confess something. Initially I entitled this chapter, "Only God can make it rain, but you can dig a ditch." However, when sharing some of these thoughts with our church staff, they pointed out that it actually didn't rain that day. In fact, in this Bible passage, Elisha almost brags about the fact that no wind or rain was needed for Jehovah God to supply the need. He can make water in the desert out of sand.

## Be a Digger for the Lord

God can handle the harvest. He is just looking for laborers. Jesus can handle the miracles, but he is waiting for the diggers.

So get your shovel out. Start digging. What if you became proactive with phone calls today? How about actually getting up really early and spending some quality time in prayer? Maybe you could go serve someone who needs assistance this evening. Perhaps you could go after loving your spouse or roommate instead of letting bitterness grow for another twenty-four-hour period.

What are you doing to tie into Jesus and his miraculous power? Our text says bringing fluid is an "easy thing" in the eyes of the Lord. He is not the problem here.

The people could have said, "We'll start digging when we see some water flowing." But that would have been too late. The prophet of God knew the power was to come from above, but the omnipotence was unleashed by people below doing what they could first.

In this book, we are primarily talking about getting back on track spiritually. That is a God thing. But the God part is triggered by the simplest acts of men and women humbling themselves to the Father's will.

So go for it today. God can send the river tomorrow.

I live in Connecticut and it has been snowing for what seems like constantly the past month (almost sixty inches in thirty days). It just started again with a storm that should last through today and tomorrow. I just prayed for safety as people travel by foot or car. Now, guess what might help my family see that prayer answered?

I need to get to work with a shovel.

You go ahead and grab one too.

GETTING BACK ON TRACK

1. How would you describe your work ethic? How would those close to you describe it? Ask them.

2. What does it mean to you to be proactive versus reactive?

3. In what ways have you prepared the circumstances in and around your life for God's miracles?

4. What are some of the greatest acts God has performed in your life past and present? As you think through these, what steps do you want to take to show him your gratitude?

# DAYS 26 & 27
# TOUCH

## Commission, Heal and Bless

"A man with leprosy came to him and begged him on his knees, 'If you are willing, you can make me clean.' Filled with compassion, Jesus reached out his hand and touched the man. 'I am willing,' he said. 'Be clean!' Immediately the leprosy left him and he was cured."

Mark 1:40–42

"At the touch of love everyone becomes a poet."

—Plato

Jesus touched a leper. It wasn't lawful. It wasn't wise. It was Jesus' way. We all need the touch of the Master's hand in our lives. We need the first touch. We need the second touch (Mark 8:22–25). We'll need many more.

The whole idea of touch or "laying on hands" is an interesting one in Scripture. Let's take a quick look at it. In Numbers 27:18–23, Moses laid his hands on Joshua to commission him as the next leader of Israel. Could he have made his choice known some other way? Sure. But in touching Joshua, Moses showed a relational affection and a planned appointment.

Jesus came along and spent quite a bit of time touching all sorts of people. In Matthew 19:13–15, he placed his hands on children and prayed for them in order to bless them (see also Mark 10:16), even in the face of others wanting him to send the kids away. In several places, Christ touched sick people. In addition to the ultra-ill like the leper mentioned above, Jesus placed his hands on a crippled woman (Luke 13:13) and those with various other diseases (Luke 4:40). He healed them all.

## The Power of Touch

Upon his departure, our Messiah allowed his apostles to perform miracles and even pass these gifts along through their human hands (Acts 8:17, Acts 19:6).

The book of Acts highlights these times of touch even more often. When the seven were appointed to serve the neglected Grecian widows in Acts 6:6, the apostles laid their hands on them. When Barnabas and Paul were commissioned to leave on the first missionary journey (Acts 13:3), the leaders of the church in Antioch laid hands on them (accompanied by prayer and fasting).

One of my favorite examples is found in Acts 9:17, when Ananias laid hands on Saul during the critical time of his conversion. It is one thing to touch someone you love, but this man was a persecutor of the church and looking to imprison or even kill followers of Christ. Touching Saul, who was about to become Paul, would have been very challenging.

I'm sure that action of touching didn't quickly leave Paul's mind because he later laid hands on the sick (Acts 28:8) and on his young evangelist protégé, Timothy (2 Timothy 1:6). An interesting verse is later written by Paul, "Don't be hasty in laying on hands" (1 Timothy 5:22). He wanted the commissioning of others in particular to be done wisely, in God's time and way.

## Take in the Message Yourself

What I am getting at is threefold. First, let Jesus touch you. Quit hiding out. Quit running away. No matter how ugly your spiritual leprosy is. Christ is a toucher. He can heal. He forgives. He loves. He changes things.

Second, you need to go after touching Jesus. I know this one is a bit metaphorical too. I thrill to the story of the woman who had been bleeding for twelve years and couldn't get a cure even though she had visited many doctors and spent all of her money (Mark 5:25–34). She snuck up behind our Savior and just touched his cloak. What phenomenal faith! She didn't need to make contact with his head or hand. She just desired the feel of the furthest away thread on his robe. And she was commended for her faith and cured from her condition.

Last, beyond that—touch others. Reach on out. Now. We live in a germophobic-frenzied world. Howie Mandell (who has an obsessive-compulsive disorder) has led a generation of Americans to not shake hands, hug or even high five anymore. The fist bump became vogue just as much to keep someone else's bacteria on their body and away from ours as to show friendship. We run from others' colds or coughs or pretty much anything. I'm not trying to circulate disease. I'm saying that the touch is a lost art that is in need of revival.

My old high school football coach rarely talked to me without a touch. He would walk up behind me and squeeze my neck or maybe come around front and put both hands on my shoulder pads. Then he would say something like this, "Jimbo, you can run the ball on that option play. You don't have to pitch it every time." His touch said as much to me as his words. He was actually saying, "That was a really dumb read. The defensive end was running out to take the tailback, and everyone alive could see you should have cut inside and run for a long gain." But his touch said it all, "You are still my quarterback. One bad play doesn't change that. Keep working. Keep learning. I'm with you all the way."

I am introverted at my core. I have learned as a disciple and especially in the ministry that I have to push beyond my nature and reach out. Long fellowship times following services were not my pattern early in life (there was a sports contest to watch on TV, a meal to eat, etc.). Now, I have the privilege and responsibility to stay, turn off the lights and lock up. But much of what I have to communicate is done through touch. I can't talk to all 400–500 people leaving our facility. I can reach out and squeeze a lot of arms on the way by, though. I can grab a hand as the communion speaker walks down, communicating, "Great job."

You can too.

I want you to touch people spiritually and physically. I want you to find your protégé and commission him or her. Take a child in your arms and bless him or her. I want you to hug a fellow Christian, shake the hand of a first-time visitor, and tackle a best friend, letting him know what he has meant in your life.

The laying on of hands was a fixture in the first-century church. Let it be in ours too. Maybe we have drifted from God a bit because we won't let Jesus touch us. All of us need more of the tenacious, coat-grabbing woman of Mark 5 in us as we run after Jesus. Now we live in an era where way too many people are untouched and distant. May it never be said of our Lord's church. May it never be said of you. Reach out and touch someone.

1. What do you learn from reading the several examples of laying on of hands in scripture?

2. How often have people touched you in positive ways in the past (both physically and emotionally)? What effect does that have on you today?

3. How can you exhibit the attitude of going after touching Jesus? What will that mean practically?

4. How can you reach out and touch others this week?

# MY FEET

# DAYS 28 & 29
# BREAKTHROUGH

## Be a Jumping Frog

When the Philistines heard that David had been anointed king over all Israel, they went up in full force to search for him, but David heard about it and went out to meet them. Now the Philistines had come and raided the Valley of Raphaim, so David inquired of God, "Shall I go and attack the Philistines? Will you hand them over to me?"

The LORD answered him, "Go, I will hand them over to you."

So David and his men went up to Baal Perazim, and there he defeated them. He said, "As waters break out, God has broken out against my enemies by my hand." So that place was Baal Perazim. The Philistines had abandoned their gods there, and David gave orders to burn them in the fire.

Once more the Philistines raided the valley, so David inquired of God again, and God answered him, "Do not go straight up, bur circle around them and attack them in front of the balsam trees. As soon as you hear the sound of marching in the tops of the balsam trees, move out to battle, because that will mean God has gone out in front of you to strike the Philistine army." So David did as God commanded him, and they struck down the Philistine army, all the way from Gibeon to Gezer.

So David's fame spread throughout every land, and the LORD made all the nations fear him.

1 Chronicles 14:8–17

"Breakdowns can create breakthroughs. Things
fall apart so things can come together."
                                    —Anonymous

A boy asked his father, "Dad, if three frogs were sitting on a limb
that hung over a pool, and one frog decided to jump off into the
pool, how many frogs would be left on the limb?"

The dad replied, "Two."

"No," the son said. "There are three frogs and one decides to
jump, how many are left?"

The dad said, "Oh, I get it. If one decides to jump, the others
would too. So there are none left."

"No," the boy said. "The answer is three. The first frog only
*decided* to jump."

Books are too often about head knowledge and decisions.
This chapter is about breakthroughs. It is about going beyond
the noble ambition in your head to see the actual miracles
of God.

## Our Enemy Keeps Coming at Us

This book would be too short to review the life of King David.
Prior to our reading today in 1 Chronicles 14, David had done
it all. He had been a shepherd, defeated Goliath, served as a
harpist for King Saul, run for his life for years, sided with the
Philistines, acted like a crazy man, failed terribly and more.

At this point in life, finally Israel was united and doing well. The
ark is soon to be securely back at home in Jerusalem (following

Uzzah's death and David's wife's sarcasm—nothing ever works too smoothly, right?). All was calm except...

Of course, the Philistines wanted to fight...again. Doesn't the devil ever leave well enough alone? The answer to that is "No." He is coming after you and me until the day we die. And what was David's reaction? He inquired of the Lord and was prepared once again to go to battle.

Battle number one was to be fought in the Valley of Rephaim or the "Valley of the Giants." This valley looms large in Jewish history. It was here that Goliath was confronted. It was this valley where fear entered Israel sitting on the edge of the Promised Land. It was here that Caleb would take on the Anakites in his later days of life.

Can I get you to stipulate to one point (I always wanted to be a lawyer and walk around and use big words but not go to an actual law school with tests, research and all)? There will *always* be battles to fight. There will never be, this side of heaven, total and complete smooth sailing.

Some of us regularly desire ease. We think this is our due as a healing time or a spiritual sabbatical. Sorry. Right now—there will always be a fight to be had.

While we moan—"Oh, my leaders"; "Oh, our church's facility"; "Oh, my arthritis" and a host of other "Oh, my's"—the enemy is conquering life after life. In verse 11, the Philistines attacked. Following that Israelite victory, they don't even give the Jews a two-verse recuperation period. In verse 13, the Bible says, "Once more the Philistines raided the valley."

I believe that every ultimate victory and the power to win it comes from God. But I think that he does it "by our hand." In fact David says in verse 11, "God has broken out against my enemies by my hand." God moves when we move. God works when we work as his hands and feet. God attacks when we attack. God is looking for someone's hand to use. Whose will it be?

## Lord of the Breakthrough

My favorite part of this story is not in the text. It is in my footnotes. Here it is. It says, "The place where the first battle was won is to this day called Baal Perazim. That name means 'the Lord who breaks out' or 'the Lord of the breakthrough.'"

Anyone needing a breakthrough out there? God specializes in them. Feel stuck? Put your hand in the hand of the man who did and does it all.

Sometimes God uses different means to bring about the breakthrough. In battle one, there was a frontal attack. In battle two, Israel snuck around the back and struck near the balsam trees. I love the "sound of marching in the tops of the balsam trees," which sure sounds like an angelic stirring to me (see also 2 Kings 6:17).

I've wandered around this subject for a while basically to say this: God can take the broken places of your life and turn them into the breakthrough places. Jesus can break through in marriages, families, hard hearts, addictions, finances and fruitlessness. I know he has different plans and places. But we serve the Almighty Lord of the Breakthrough.

I have heard that the Philistines are mentioned 286 times in the Bible. They are perhaps the chief rival and general bully to the Israelite people. In this chapter, it is exciting to see Israel chasing them all the way from Gibeon to Gezer (and with the young bucks to the old geezers).

The Valley of Giants will never be mentioned again in the biblical record of Israel. Actually, giants themselves don't show up in any subsequent stories. Why not? Because God is the Lord of the breakthrough perhaps.

Our Father won many physical battles in Old Testament times. He can win plenty of spiritual ones today. Jesus said, "I will build my church," and he will. He can change us. He can mend what is broken in us. Let him. Work with him.

Everything doesn't have to be breaking up. With God, a better life can be breaking through.

## GETTING BACK ON TRACK

1. What is presently breaking down in your life? How are you dealing with it?

2. How have you seen the devil work on you and others in
   the past?

3. What has God changed most in you over the course of
   your life?

4. What spiritual breakthrough will you pray about and fight
   for during these forty days?

# DAY 30

# ACT

## Clean Up Your Messes

Designate a place outside the camp where you can go to relieve yourself. As part of your equipment have something to dig with, and when you relieve yourself, dig a hole and cover up your excrement. For the LORD your God moves about in your camp to protect you and to deliver your enemies to you. Your camp must be holy, so that he will not see among you anything indecent and turn away from you.

Deuteronomy 23:12–14

"This mess is a place."—Anonymous

I have been reading the Bible for many years. I'm not that young either. So if you had asked me for most of my life if the Holy Scriptures covered what to do when you go to the bathroom, I would have quickly and authoritatively said, "No way." I would have been wrong.

Recently I stumbled across the verse from Deuteronomy printed above. I never thought I would write a book. If I did, I certainly didn't think I would have a chapter in it on going to the bathroom. This text helps me believe in the authenticity of God's Book. No man, woman or child would put this part in the Holy Writ, right?

Why would God take up valuable lines in the most important book ever written to discuss relieving ourselves? I'm not sure, but let me venture a guess. This may be the most dramatic passage ever put to papyrus in describing the importance of cleaning up our messes.

I'm not a big camper. But if I were, I'd like the campground cleaned just as Moses described in Deuteronomy. Who wants to walk around stepping into messes—their own or someone else's? Bury that stuff. Take a shovel. Clean up your messes.

That seems to make good sense when it comes to hygiene. I just wish we would understand it is every bit as important in the rest of life.

**Deal with Your Own Messes**

I can't tell you the number of people I cross paths with who do not want to deal with their messes. For some, there is a string of broken relationships, conflict and hurt feelings. For others, there are bill collectors at every turn. There is the thief or the sex addict or the lazy sluggard...and they all have stuff lying around undealt with from the past and the present.

Jesus stated this same point slightly differently in Matthew 5:25: "Settle matters quickly." The Alcoholics Anonymous Big Book says, "Make amends." God told thousands of camping Israelites, "Clean up your messes."

It is really easy to be paralyzed with fear. We're afraid one day our wife will find out about "it." We cross our fingers and hope that God will be gracious and we won't reap the repercussions from our stuff. Perhaps we even sit and cry about it all.

There once was a prodigal son. He wasted his family inheritance, lived the opposite of the way he should have and ended up miserable. He didn't just cry, though maybe it started there. He didn't just sit around in pig poop. At some point, he got up and started going back to his dad's house. He *acted*. Exposing his sin. Apologizing. Being sneered at by an older brother. Those weren't easy things to go through. They were hard. But they weren't as hard as his messed-up life away from his father.

One passage that has always stood out to me is Proverbs 13:15b, which says, "The way of the unfaithful is hard." Too often I can moan and groan about how hard the life of a disciple is. Really? Okay, in some ways I suppose. But Scripture actually says it is being unrighteous or unfaithful that is the hardest way to go. Our sinful lives are what cause messes and mess ups everywhere we turn.

### What If You Did?

So, what if you went after cleaning up your messes? What if you confessed the truth about what has really been going on in your life? What if you got the prayers and help of others and even tasted some spiritual healing (James 5:16)? What if you believed the part about "walking in the light" and went after that road wholeheartedly and moved away from the dark back-alleys of skating by?

What if you got up and did something for and with God today?

When I was young, I often played with an older kid who lived down the street from me. He led me into a little trouble from time to time. I seemed occasionally eager to follow. One day we were throwing rocks at a street sign (yes, a brilliant pastime for a future preacher). He missed the sign on one fateful throw, and the rock smacked with great force into a car driving by...and it was a really nice, expensive car.

My first thought was, "Let's run for it!!" My buddy, not known for his spirituality, did run. But he didn't run away; he ran to the car, whose driver had pulled over on the side of the road. My friend apologized profusely while the angry man cursed and screamed. I followed, watched, trembled and waited for the police to come take us away. They didn't.

For some reason, after unleashing his anger, the man got back into his car and drove on down the road with a large new dent in his nice ride. I learned an amazing lesson from a rough-around-the-edges guy that day. Clean up your messes. Don't run from them. Don't wish them away. Don't blame someone else.

**Go After It!**

There is a parable in the Bible about a five-talent man who gained five more talents (a denomination of money) for his master. There was a two-talent man who gained two additional talents for his master as well. There was a final one-talent man who did nothing. He didn't lose his money. He didn't gain any. And God was angry. He was displeased. He wanted man #3 to try, to seek, to ask, to knock.

We've all heard the old adage that it is easier to direct a moving object than a stationary one. Get up and act. Do something. God will use it. Clean your messes up. You and many others will be forever thankful that you did.

1. How does your bedroom look right now? Your office? The kitchen? Does this reveal anything about your character to you?

2. How do you do at settling matters quickly?

3. Are you quick or slow to apologize? Why?

4. Do you believe that it is the way of the faithful or the un-faithful that is hard? Why?

5. Do you tend to blame others for your messes? If so, who and why?

6. What can you do today to begin to deal with life's messes (my wife wants me to start in the bedroom)?

# DAYS 31 & 32
# FLEE

## A Way-Out Mentality

No temptation has seized you except what is common to man. And God is faithful; he will not let you be tempted beyond what you can bear. But when you are tempted, he will also provide a way out so that you can stand up under it.

1 Corinthians 10:13

"It is easier to stay out than to get out."

—Mark Twain

In Proverbs 7:6–27, one of the scariest stories of the Bible is told. It begins innocently enough. The author looks out from his balcony window and notices a young man walking down the street. But as the story continues, it reads like a steamy romance novel.

"He was going down the street near her corner...at twilight as the day was fading, as the dark of night set in." Then the woman comes out to meet the young man "with crafty intent."

At this early point in the story, nothing too bad has happened. Men are allowed to walk down streets. Women can step outside for a little fresh air. However, anyone looking from the window or reading this proverb can tell that spiritual devastation is on its way. Disaster is screaming down the tracks like a runaway locomotive. The crash will be loud, and its impact will destroy much.

*133*

"With persuasive words she led him astray; she seduced him with her smooth talk. All at once he followed her like an ox going to the slaughter...little knowing it will cost him his life.... Her house is a highway to the grave, leading down to the chambers of death."

## Where Is Your Path Headed?

Everyone is on a path that goes somewhere. Most of us have good intentions. We want great families, healthy dating relationships, and imitatable lives. But you must know this. The road you are going down trumps your intentions. The way your feet walk will overcome a noble desire or two.

Though this young man is thinking he is "hot" and living the life of a "pro athlete," the real song playing on the stereo is the theme from *Jaws* (sorry, this movie was released in 1975—insert some more contemporary example from the past thirty-five years if you wish). The grave, the chamber of death, hell itself—this is no place for anyone. It's not imaginary. It's not a cartoon.

Pornography, which started out as "just a little fun that everyone does," ends up with something being released in your brain that programs your body for the future. Pornography becomes addictive, enslaving and depressing. Watch out on this "boys will be boys" path you start down.

Just chatting with that nice guy from work who is sensitive to you seems harmless. Your husband at home doesn't seem to notice you much or care about your needs. Conversation is no sin, you say. Be careful where you wander. Roads lead someplace.

Proverbs 27:12 says, "The prudent see danger and take refuge; but the simple keep going and suffer for it." Sadly, it is always easier to keep going than to stop and turn around. However, if the bridge is out ahead, you had better use the brakes and do a U-turn.

We borrow, borrow and borrow some more—leveraging debt for a certain lifestyle. That is a boulevard of broken dreams. We smoke or drink excessively and/or eat incessantly. We are heading down Angst Avenue.

2 Timothy 2:22 says very clearly, "Flee youthful lusts." Run away. Put your head down and sprint in the opposite direction. The young man in Proverbs ended up wishing he had done that. The sex addict now says "Amen" but feels deep down it is too late.

If I may be so bold: Quit staying up by yourself watching late-night television or playing around on the Internet. Stop flirting at work. Cut up the credit cards. What does it mean for you to flee from sin? Write down your own ideas.

## Don't Walk Where It Is Slippery

I heard about a man who decided to go on a diet. He cut sweets out of his menu. He did pretty well until one day he arrived at his office with a huge coffee cake in his hands, oozing with icing and nuts. "Aren't you on a diet?" one of his co-workers questioned.

"Oh, this is different," replied the man. "You see, this morning I was driving by the bakery and I said to God, 'God, if you want me to stop, please allow there to be a parking spot in front of the bakery.' And, sure enough, after seven times around the block, there was a spot."

No more rationalizing. If you don't want to fall, don't walk where it is slippery.

Recently I had a Bible study with a young man on the topic of sin. He confessed an addiction. I quickly guessed alcohol, drugs or sex. He said, "No—video games." I asked what exactly that meant. He said that it meant playing video games about three-to-six hours every day. In fact, he pulled a game from his coat pocket and informed me that he always keeps something on him in case he has free time.

I challenged him to give up video games for a week for starters. Then someone who was with us had the nerve to say, "What do all of us need to give up for a week to show God that he really is #1 in our lives?"

One said "technology." Another "coffee." I took "television." Later, upon consulting my wife, I added sodas to the Jesus dare.

Perhaps you think I am off topic now. I certainly wouldn't put that past me. But I think we all are much too focused on "me." And when what I want becomes central, I begin to move down a road away from Christ. I think that is what temptation is. Does one coffee do that? No. Is being on a computer wrong? Can't I be friendly at work with someone of the opposite sex? Good questions. My question back would be: What direction are you traveling? What road are you on?

God wants you to have fun, but sin is dark, bad stuff and has consequences. Temptation is what leads us there. Walk down well-lit spiritual roads today. When temptation comes calling, remember first of all that it is better to "stay out" than to "get out." But when you are "in" the throes of temptation, *run*! Kick it into high gear, unashamedly. Flee. Your eternal life does depend on it.

GETTING BACK ON TRACK

1. Explain how Satan tempts you. What are his customized tricks and schemes?

2. What are your strongest temptations? How well are you running from those at present?

3. How well do you do at handling financial matters? If improvement is needed, who could you get great advice from?

4. What are you addicted to? Is there anything you would have
   a hard time giving up for one week? If so, consider fasting
   from that in the week ahead.

5. Why is sin bad?

6. What are the joys of fleeing from evil?

# MY LIPS

# DAYS 33 & 34

# PRAY

## Busting Loose from the 90%

"I tell you the truth, if you have faith as small a mustard seed, you can say to this mountain, 'Move from here to there' and it will move. Nothing will be impossible for you."

Matthew 17:20

"Courage is fear that has said its prayers."
—Dorothy Bernard

I realized something that really saddened me a few months ago. I came to the conclusion that 90% of the things I pray for would happen anyway, even if I didn't pray.

I began to retrace the words of my prayers. They were way too benign, humdrum, standard and safe.

"Dear Lord, bless my wife and daughters. Help them to have a good day. Keep them safe. Please don't let it rain for the outdoor service we have planned tomorrow. Keep me safe as I drive around to appointments today. Help us reach budget in our giving. Guide us. Guard us. Direct us. Help the elders to have wisdom, the deacons to serve you and..."

No wonder I fall asleep in some of my prayer times. I think God must too.

Now, I don't think there is anything inherently wrong with any of the requests above. I think it is fine to pray for the little things, even the mundane things of life. I am okay with general prayers. They don't all have to be microscopically specific.

But I began to think that my neighbor who doesn't even pray has had a safe family over the past few years. He has had decent days. Sometimes it rains on him and other times it doesn't (by the way—it rained the last Sunday that we had an outdoor service planned and we moved it inside...the world didn't stop spinning and all seemed to go fine). He's had no car wrecks lately and seems to be in better financial shape than I am. The elders God has blessed us with haven't lost their wisdom, which I am thankful for. Our servants seem to mostly keep on serving. That's fine.

I think you get my point. I pray like I really don't have to, except that the Bible says I should.

## What Are You Praying For?

So my question is—what are you praying for *big*? For that matter, what are you working on in life that is *large*?

In Matthew 6:31–33, Jesus says that we should not worry about the little things. He says that is what the pagans run after. I just looked up "pagan" in the dictionary to see if there is a nicer word to use. There isn't. The corresponding word is "heathen." God seems to be mocking us. Perhaps he is even making fun of me. He's saying, "Jimmy, in the way you pray you are no better than those who don't even believe."

What am I praying for that would not happen unless God was totally here and involved? Those would be the prayers I would pray emotionally, relentlessly and faithfully. Do we think God would be annoyed by big prayers or maybe honored because we saw him as immense and all-powerful?

What if the size of my prayers tells my kids about the size of my God? What if the size of my prayers tells the church about the dimensions of the One I say I believe in?

Once a month in our congregation, we write out prayer requests. This allows us to pray for and with each other regularly. Sadly, what I realized is that each time we do that, I pause and think for awhile about what to write down. What does that tell you if I can't really even think of anything quickly? It probably isn't something too big. It doesn't seem like it will be that scary or awe-inspiring.

I want to start praying, talking and living **BIG**.

**Teach Us to Pray**

What would you say or do if a friend asked you to teach him to pray? Would you give him the A-C-T-S (adoration-confession-thanksgiving-supplication)? I love that acronym and pray it often. Probably what I would do is invite that friend to go on a prayer walk me. That would be fine, and there is power in two or more together (Matthew 18:20).

Do you know what? Someone did ask Jesus to teach him to pray. It happened in Luke 11:1. And you probably know what Christ did, right? God's Son said what we call "The Lord's Prayer," in verses 2–4. This passage is shorter than the more familiar parallel one in Matthew 6:9–13. In Luke 11, Jesus said what in English takes only four sentences. In the New International Version it is thirty-four words. My daughter just read me the prayer and I timed it—ten seconds in length reading slowly (by the way, I'm not saying any of my daughters are slow; they are all beautiful and brilliant and...maybe a little over-sensitive that I might embarrass them in this book).

Here's something I learned recently. Jesus didn't just tell us in Luke 11 about a prayer. He also taught us the heart of praying, and we hardly ever discuss it in the context of this man's question. We read the prayer and stop. Luke didn't stop there.

In Luke 11:5–13, the gospel physician keeps going, very probably in the same time continuum by stating, "Then he said to them...." What follows is one of the strangest stories about God possible. Jesus compares his own loving Father to a sleepy, annoyed, agitated friend. He speaks of a door-knocker at midnight who wakes everyone up in their Middle Eastern home (usually one large room where all slept, not multiple bedrooms on different levels) and wouldn't stop banging until food was brought out.

First please note that he is door-knocking at night for someone else—not himself. Then the Bible says, in essence, "Look at this guy's boldness. God really loves bold asking!"

In making almost the same point in Luke 18:1–8 later, God is compared to a wicked, unjust judge. What? Why? I'd never do that in a sermon. Jesus did. The passage concludes with these statements, "And will not God bring about justice for his chosen ones who cry out to him day and night...? However, when the Son of Man comes, will he find faith on the earth?"

God is looking for radical faith in our prayer! He wants to see if we will cry out day and night or just mumble a few things a time or two and then get perturbed because what we are entitled to isn't happening or at least isn't happening quickly enough for our liking.

We pray too tame and too polite. People came after God in the Old Testament. In the New Testament these stories show us individuals banging on doors late at night and crying out, begging, day after day. Maybe Jehovah God said, "Finally, someone is asking BIG!"

My biggest, most consistent and loudest prayers for the past seventeen years have regarded my family and the Hartford church. As I look back at what has happened (and my sight is not God's for sure), I see the most amazing blessings in the areas of my family and the congregation here. I have prayed in a very mellow way for the gospel to spread throughout other parts of the world and for unexplainable missions contributions to be collected among our members. And in my small and quiet prayers for these things, I have seen small things happen.

Let me be quick to say that God and his moving do not revolve all around me. But I must say that my prayer life comes from me, and it has been way too small, short-sighted, weak, boring and safe.

## Pray Radical Prayers

I decided to try out this new, radical conviction I had gained in 2010. I focused on three miraculous areas of prayer. These were scary prayers for me. I believed that only God could make these come about, and his doing so was not guaranteed to happen in a day. I'll share two of the three prayer requests with you (the third area has been amazing too, but remember—I'm trying not to embarrass any of my four precious girls).

I began to pray almost daily for miraculous financial growth in our congregation. In the past, I might have been afraid to ask this. But, as I see so much that must be done in Connecticut, New England and the world, I could hold back no longer. We need a larger facility or facilities. We have to put on more staff and train them. In our own small state we have innumerable cities that must be planted with disciples who will share the good news. Think of your own state or nation. Connecticut must have churches in Waterbury, Torrington, New Haven, Danbury, and many more cities. You haven't heard of most of these, but

God has and he cares. We need some money and people to get there. So does your church.

So I prayed and thought maybe God could move a couple of millionaires into our congregation. I waited. And waited. And in six months several people moved away who were strong givers. This wasn't really working, until...

One morning at an elders' and evangelists' meeting, two of our elders proposed that we raise the budget for our contribution 15% per week. I thought they had gone loopy. Perhaps the early 6:15 AM meeting had slowed their brain cells. Maybe they had missed the news that our country was in one of the worst economic downturns ever. No, couldn't be—one of these two elders had recently been without a job for about a year. They knew.

They were just walking by faith instead of by sight. They were asking our church to do something miraculous with our finances so that we could find a larger facility, add new staff and plant new churches. They proposed this, and our church got fired up beyond my imagination. They didn't want to give just for giving's sake, but they would gladly give to see God's dreams come true in our state and the world.

As I write this many months later, our contribution has been much higher than 15% more per week. I'm still stunned. I don't get it. My prayers weren't answered my way, but my prayers have been answered. Now I have to start praying even bigger.

My other radical request was for God to save souls in the Conard High School community in which I live. My three daughters have all attended high school at this West Hartford school. The youngest of our three is now a sophomore and there is not a lot of time left to take advantage of her connections to see people brought to Jesus. My daughters' hearts for God have always blown me away. They came on a small church planting (only two had been born) and have all either been in a nonexistent teen ministry or a very small one. They have followed Jesus anyway and touched many along the way. Conard High has disciples in it today as I write and even an after-school, weekly Bible Talk.

But it's our last round and I want to see something mega-miraculous (redundant I know, but let's go with it). So I began to pray and am still praying daily. I wanted (and still do) many families to start flowing into our church services and asking for Bible studies. It didn't happen. A few, mainly moms and daughters, have come and we're still working it...but I was missing my miracle.

Except...one day out of nowhere, a college student in our ministry, Kyle, said he was studying the Bible with this guy named Daeshawn who went to Conard the year before. Now Daeshawn was a big man on campus in high school (in some good and some not-so-good ways—I won't confess his sin here). Long story short: Daeshawn became a Christian. Not too long after that, April, who had just graduated from Conard became a disciple too. Then, more kids who were Conard grads started filing in. And the story continues. Trust me, this crew is on fire.

Now, God didn't and hasn't answered my prayer my way. But He certainly has proven himself faithful. Now I have to start praying even scarier prayers.

What is the point? Mostly it is to pray. You can pray for anything. I will not complain if you are talking to God. But I'd like to challenge you to try to freak God out with some requests. I have found that you cannot do it. In fact, my new conviction is that these are the types of requests a father loves to hear from his kids.

My daughter wanted Jolly Ranchers for a car trip. I got her two bags. My wife often wants a small Coke slushie. I spring for the medium for her on occasion because I love her and want her happy!

Ask big and God will come through larger. Request minor miracles and God will raise the dead.

## GETTING BACK ON TRACK

1. What do you think Dorothy Bernard's quote means: "Courage is fear that has said its prayers"?

2. How is your prayer life? Why?

3. What are you praying for that is big and scary? If not much, what can you add to the list?

4. What attitude (that goes beyond just words) does God desire in your prayers?

5. What do the illustrations of God in Luke 11 and 18 teach us about his character?

# Days 35 & 36

# Confess

## Open Up or You Will Stay Shut Down

He who conceals his sins does not prosper,
> but whoever confesses and renounces them
> finds mercy.

Proverbs 28:13

"Should we all confess our sins to one another,
we would all laugh at one another for our lack of
originality."—Kahlil Gibran

In the fellowship of churches of which I am part, we make the "good confession" before a person's baptism. This practice is taken from the Romans 10:9 scripture reference which says that first-century believers stated, "Jesus is Lord," as opposed to the Roman cry of the day that "Caesar is Lord."

At one particular baptism that I witnessed, the brothers didn't coach the baptizee too well. Following some emotional sharing and the dramatic question, "What is your good confession?" the about-to-be young Christian said, "Lying, lust, shoplifting..." We stopped him as quickly as we could. That seemed more like the bad confession than the good one.

People have been shutting down confessions for a long, long time in churches.

I grew up wanting others to know all of the good about me they could, and my strongest desire on earth was to hide from them anything bad. I certainly didn't want my parents to know the real stuff. Of course, I had no desire for any preacher to be informed. There were certain subjects I even went to great lengths to hide from my friends. But it was all still there. And it haunted me. Who would find it out? When? How would they react?

The Bible actually has a lot to say on this topic. Here is just a sampling.

> Luke 12:2—"There is nothing concealed that will not be disclosed or hidden that will not be made known."
>
> Proverbs 10:9—The man of integrity walks securely, but he who takes crooked paths will be found out.
>
> Ecclesiastes 12:14—For God will bring every deed into judgment including every hidden thing, whether good or evil.
>
> Numbers 32:23—You may be sure that your sin will find you out.
>
> Matthew 3:6—Confessing their sins, they were baptized by him in the Jordan River.
>
> James 5:16—Therefore confess your sins to each other and pray for each other so that you may be healed. The prayer of a righteous man is powerful and effective.

The family of churches I am part of has many flaws, weaknesses and sins. We are far from perfect. But one trait I have never witnessed or heard of anywhere else is radical, consistent openness by the membership. Certainly this is not consistently true with every one of us, and that is why I am writing this chapter.

However, the call to one-another confession (not confession to the priest; not "smile and look pious" while saying nothing; not eking out 1/100 of what is really going on) has, will and is changing my life on an ongoing basis.

Why should we confess our sins? I can kind of see the women doing it. They like those bonding, emotional moments, right? But the fellas? It's just embarrassing for us.

**Prayers and Help of Others**

In James 5:16, it says that first of all we get the prayers and help of other people when we confess. When I share with you my struggles with impatience, cowardice or whatever, instead of judgment and laughter I have found that I get a set or two of eyeballs which communicate understanding. Men close to God tell me of their similar struggles (victories and failures) and how they are fighting the battle too.

We then commit to praying for each other. None of us knows how powerful just that act alone is. Following verse 16, James reminds us of the story of Elijah, a man just like us. He prayed that it wouldn't rain for three years and it didn't. He then prayed it would rain again and it did. In context, I wonder what would happen if we fervently prayed for each other's battles with the devil. I'm guessing pretty dramatic stories would be told more often.

**Healing**

But beyond the help and prayers, the Holy Spirit mentions a second reason to open up. It is "so you will be healed." I am convinced that sin is worse than cancer. Sin destroys beyond the body. If a patient with cancer is told by his operating doctor following surgery that 50% of the cancer cells were removed, there would be depression not celebration. The other cells will continue to annihilate him.

People don't just need to mumble about probably not being as obedient to their parents as they could have been or shading the truth on a few occasions. We need to get it all out with someone we trust and let its horrific acid eat away the dining room table we are sitting around, but not continue to decimate our soul for another day.

What is most embarrassing? What do you least want to share? Get that out. Start with it. You don't get healed without heading there. But what if it is really bad and could affect my marriage or my job? Let me help you—it is already affecting your family, your church, your occupation and everything else. When ensnared by secret sin, you have closed down, shut up and begun to exist rather than really love, live and give.

Over the course of many years in the ministry, I have heard every sin confessed found in Galatians 5:19–21, many more, and a few that we North Americans have invented in the 21st century. I respect far more the man or woman sharing these deep, sensitive offenses over the religious "chat about the weather and sports" hypocrite. Which are you?

There is hardly a week that goes by that someone does not ask me how I am doing with lust. I have asked them to, given them total permission. Why is that? I have a gorgeous wife. I have three beautiful daughters. Why or how could I ever be tempted? Every man reading this knows exactly how (sorry ladies, we'll get to you soon).

I have dealt with many anger issues in my life. All my friends growing up actually viewed me as mild-mannered. Sure, in public. I've had more than one occasion where my four favorite women have circled up the chairs in our living room to tell me how my anger has made them feel. So, I share that with other men and ask for their prayers, accountability and help.

I could go on...and on.

Fellas—Do you lie? Are you lazy? Are you a bully at home (I'm not talking about in your own eyes; how about the view of your wife and children?)?

Ladies—Do you slice and dice people with your tongue at a moment's notice through gossip or slander? Do you deprive your husband of sexual intimacy (in direct rebellion to God as stated in 1 Corinthians 7:5)? Do you lust after men (either those guys with the hot look or—if you are married—the ones who seem more understanding and sympathetic than the guy you got stuck with)?

The truth is—you sin, a lot. I do too. There are sins of commission and others of omission (James 4:17). There are iniquities on the Internet, telephone and TV. There are transgressions at school, home, work and on vacation. Will we ever be like Jesus? Only if we open up.

Most people don't easily change. Let's say this too: Openness is ultimately not the cure-all. You can share "it" and still not do anything about it. But my experience with people and God's word also tells me that those not confessing anything are not changing much.

I am all for confessing our sins to God. He is the One who forgives, not man. But everyone reading this needs a brother or sister or two in his or her life listening, sharing back, praying and being a part of Christ's plan to get out of the addictions, pits and hell-holes we have been in.

One well-known preacher once said, "Most churches survive because everyone keeps a polite distance from each other. We keep our sermons short and our conversations superficial."

And here is my editorial comment: It is killing people, not helping them.

Who will be brave today? Who will day after day really go after being like Jesus? Open up now, not later. You will be eternally thankful that you did.

## GETTING BACK ON TRACK

1. In just the few verses cited in this chapter, what is God saying about the way we should deal with our sin? Why?

2. Which best describes you regarding confession of sin—smiles and looks pious, ekes out a little every now and then, or is very vulnerable and an open book? Explain your answer.

3. Is there something you should confess today? Will you?

4. What are the blessings of confession you have seen and felt in your life?

# DAYS 37 & 38

# VOW

## The Ones Who Get the Last Laugh

> How can I repay the LORD
>     for all his goodness to me?
> I will lift up the cup of salvation
>     and call on the name of the LORD.
> I will fulfill my vows to the LORD
>     in the presence of all his people.
>                                     Psalm 116:12–14

"'Tis not many oaths that makes the truth, but the plain single vow that is vowed true."
—William Shakespeare

In 1932 the freshman football team at Stanford University was undefeated. However, the varsity did not fare so well. They finished 6-4-1 and suffered the school's fifth straight loss to their archrival, the University of Southern California. Following the season, the legendary Pop Warner quit and moved to Temple University because he thought Stanford's admission policy was too stringent to ever compete for a championship.

Warner was a good football coach, but on this one he was dead wrong. The Monday following the varsity season, freshman quarterback Frank Alustiza gathered the first-year players around. He proclaimed, "USC will never do that to our team. We'll never lose to the Trojans." As the story goes, another team member yelled out, "Let's make that a vow." They did.

*157*

And from 1933 until 1935, Stanford played in three straight Rose Bowls. Their overall record was 25-4-2. They never lost to the USC Trojans. In fact, five of the fellas who affectionately became known as the "Vow Boys" in Stanford lore made All American over the course of their college football years.

## Vow-Making in the Bible

The Bible has a lot to say about vow-making. First, there is the bad news. Perhaps Jephthah is best known for making a rash vow. In Judges 11:30–31, he asks for God's help in defeating the Ammonites and then promises to give up the first thing out of his front door upon returning home. Unfortunately, you know, it was his daughter.

The author of Proverbs 20 speaks back to Jephthah but also forward to us as he states in verse 25, "It is a trap for a man to dedicate something rashly and only later to consider his vows." Psalm 66:13–14 gives us more insight as it speaks to mankind's penchant to vow something to God in the middle of our own personal trouble.

One might think it would be easier just to never promise or vow anything. However, that is not the tone of scripture. Over and over, the Bible tells us to fulfill our vows (Psalm 50:14); fulfill them day after day (Psalm 61:8); and to even make vows which you will later follow through with (Isaiah 19:21).

In Malachi 1:14, Jehovah calls "cursed" anyone who vows to give the best of his herd and yet sacrifices a blemished animal instead. God was not against the vowing. He merely wanted the walk to follow the talk.

There's a big "wow" vowing verse in Ecclesiastes 5:4–6. It says,

> When you make a vow to God, do not delay in fulfilling it. He has no pleasure in fools; fulfill your

vow. It is better not to vow than to make a vow and not fulfill it. Do not let your mouth lead you into sin. And do not protest to the temple messenger, "My vow was a mistake." Why should God be angry at what you say and destroy the work of your hands? Much dreaming and many words are meaningless. Therefore stand in awe of God.

## Breaking Vows

We live in a world today where many are quick to break vows. Marriage is no longer for better or for worse, in sickness and in health, and till death do us part (this problem is not just outside the church, by the way). It seems these days couples come with a promise to be together until she gets really annoying or he loses a job or some other issue arrives on the scene.

People make vows to Jesus in the waters of baptism after counting the cost (Luke 14:25–35). They say nothing will turn them around. They proudly proclaim Christ as Lord for all to hear for life and, for that matter, eternity. But sometimes within a few days, when the winds begin to blow a little, their spiritual house comes crashing down. Maybe the parents made a bit of an issue. Perhaps an old girlfriend showed up. In some cases, academics or the career or just about anything calls, and way too many jettison the oath made to the Sovereign God over all.

Psalm 5:9 speaks of people outside of God's covenant and says, "Not a word from their mouth can be trusted." How about your word?

## Be a 'Vow Boy' or 'Vow Girl'

I'm all for making promises. And, by the way, these don't have to be accompanied by swearing (Matthew 5:34–37); just let your "yes" be your "yes." Tell your kids the truth—that you will be there for them no matter what—and live up to it when they disappoint you. Fulfill the marriage vows you made in the presence of many people. Say "yes" to Jesus and mean "yes" even when the going gets tough.

Who are the "vow boys and girls" in the 21st century? It must be disciples of Jesus Christ. Make some commitment today and a promise to draw closer to God. Vow to get back on track. Now go for it.

Here's one other interesting note regarding the Stanford Vow Boys. Pop Warner, who virtually all football players have heard of even now over seventy years later, left as Stanford's coach. Any idea who the new coach was during Stanford football's glory days of the Vow Boys? It was Tiny Thornhill. That's not exactly the most menacing of names, and I'm guessing very few have heard of him.

We all respond to leaders. I am very thankful for the family, friends, staff members, elders and wives, deacons and wives, and small group leaders who have influenced my life. But in this instance, it doesn't seem like the leader was the key. The vow and the forcefulness that went into following it was. I hope your church leaders are on fire for God. I hope you thrill to learning from them and follow wholeheartedly. However, it really starts with *you*. You must make the vow. You must tenaciously be a man or woman of your word.

I'm also hoping there are a host of spiritual vow boys in heaven one day. I'm praying there will be many other guys and girls from all over the world with the same nickname. By the way, the one other moniker for this group of freshmen turned champions was the "laughing boys." They must have had a lot of fun. Fulfill your vows and you definitely get the last laugh.

1. What are some rash promises you have made in life? What have those taught you?

2. What are the spiritual vows you have made (to God, spouse, others)? How are you doing in fulfilling them?

3. Can other people trust your words?

4. Are you reliable? How can you grow in this area?

# Days 39 & 40

# SHARE

## On the Way

It happened that as *he made his way* toward Jerusalem, he crossed over the border between Samaria
and Galilee. As he entered a village, ten men, all lepers, met him. They kept their distance but raised their
voices, calling out, "Jesus, Master, have mercy on us!"

Taking a good look at them, he said, "Go, show
yourselves to the priests." They went, and while still
*on their way*, became clean.

One of them, when he realized that he was
healed, turned around and came back, shouting his
gratitude, glorifying God. He kneeled at Jesus' feet,
so grateful. He couldn't thank him enough—and he
was a Samaritan.

Jesus said, "Were not ten healed? Where are
the nine? Can none be found to come back and give
glory to God except this outsider?" Then he said to
him, "Get up. On your way. Your faith has healed
and saved you."

Luke 17:11–19 (The Message, emphasis mine)

"It is not our business to make the message ac-
ceptable, but to make it available. We are not to
see that they like it, but that they get it."

—Vance Havner

What runs through your mind when you are on your way to
the store? Seems obvious, right? You're getting your list in your

*163*

head and trying to park in the best spot possible. What are you thinking about when you are on your way to the post office? Yes, wondering if the line will be long. You may be questioning whether to pay with cash or credit card.

Jesus was amazing "on his way." He was always thinking about the Father's business. He always had his eyes and heart alert to help others. It didn't matter if it was a rich but small man in a tree, an immoral woman at the water cooler or lepers. Jesus was ready "on his way." It was when much of his best stuff got done.

## The Ten Lepers

The story of the ten lepers is an amazing one. No miraculous healing of our Messiah was routine, but typically Jesus touched or spit or made mud. At least he would say something that made good common sense like, "Rise and walk."

In this case, from a distance, Jesus said something that seemed ludicrous. He stated to a group that included a Samaritan, "Go show yourself to the priest." You can go read about this dictate in Leviticus 13–14 for more information, but suffice it to say that when someone was cleansed, the priest allowed the new "clean" individual to re-enter public life.

There was one problem. Jesus said to go to the priest, and the men looked down at their bodies still littered with leprosy. To go before the priest in this state would be laughable for most. For the Samaritan, it could cost him his life.

One lesson for us to learn is the lesson of faith. When Jesus says something, what is your reaction? Do you analyze it, constantly question it or flatly rebel? When you are humbled by leprosy, you will do anything. These ten did and they were cleansed. We don't and remain in our trouble. But it all began in this story because Jesus was on his way with his eyes open.

Because Jesus started with an "on his way" mentality, we now read about the ten going "on their way" to the priest. They were leprous as they left but "on their way" they were cleansed.

One of the big problems in most churches is that much material hits people's heads and hearts but it never makes it all the way down into lives. We teach on prayer. We read books about it. We look up famous quotations. But do we pray? We discuss evangelism in small group settings and share a lot of good points, after which we all nod and say, "That's right!" But do we share our faith consistently on our way? Miracles don't tend to happen in the classroom. They happen "on our way" to a city, to the dry cleaners, to the church service and to about anywhere.

## One Leper Leaping

Our story concludes with one leper being sent on his way after saying "thank you" to Jesus for his healing.

How about one more side point? Did you know that unexpressed gratitude comes across as ingratitude? Don't you think all ten lepers were thankful? If I could interview them now, they would each probably point to Jesus' healing as the best day of their lives. However, they didn't say it, and Jesus was not pleased. Their one mention in scripture is a negative one, not because they didn't feel the right thing, but because they said nothing.

Every now and then my wife feels unappreciated for her acts of service to me. I can't understand that! I eat and gain weight and wear those clothes she irons with a smile. How can she not know of my gratitude? It is because unexpressed thanksgiving comes across as ingratitude—maybe the last thing we intend to communicate. If you think it, say it. If you have been too quiet with thanks, share some today.

And now back to our Samaritan leper—he was sent by Jesus on his way. That is where all of us are sent once we have been healed by him. We should now with sincere gratitude have our eyes opened wide to the needs of others—physical, emotional and spiritual.

I fail at this more often than I succeed, but every now and then God helps me stumble across the Jesus way. I went to Best Buy a while back with a computer problem. I do not like computer problems. I had to stand in a long line to get help. I don't like lines...even short ones. Over the course of my hour in the store, a man behind me and I started a conversation. He visited church service the following Sunday. Now he is studying the Bible. That was my best computer problem ever. And even if he hadn't shown any openness, it is a joy to be Christ's ambassador while I am on my way.

So in a few minutes I will be on my way to get gas. What will I find at the station? Who will be there in the car nearby? What will I hear being discussed in the line? Who will need my help, my voice? I don't know, but it's time to find out.

You too. Be on your way today.

## GETTING BACK ON TRACK

1. What is the biggest challenge for you in sharing your faith? How can you overcome this obstacle?

2. Do you have "fishing holes" that you frequent in your neighborhood or city? If not, can you find some? How do your conversations go in these places?

3. Will you speak up today for Jesus? How can you make this the natural habit and flow of your life?

4. What are the joys you have found in sharing with others?

# Epilogue

# Back on Track for God

In the Introduction, you read about a train that was on track, going somewhere, chugging and hauling, getting the job done, and then it happened—a derailment that was never expected. It looked hopeless for that train—it would never be useful again. Its purpose was destroyed. No future in sight.

But then we realized the story wasn't really over. There was life after death. There was retrofitting. There was hope.

We are that train. You are. I am. We are all in need of spiritual retrofitting. Daily. Now.

Let me share a paragraph from the Introduction:

> Most of us don't dramatically dart away, but we sure do drift. Then there comes a day when we say, "How did I end up here?" This book is an effort to help some find the way back to the Father. But beyond that, it is an attempt to help us all reignite our passions, retrofit our plans and return wholeheartedly to the gospel train of God's purposes.

After spending forty days considering who God is and who he calls us to be, what is your renewed goal in life? What do you want to commit yourself to from today until the day you die? Write it down. Go back to it (and to your responses to the questions in this book) when you feel the need to renew your focus, to get back on the tracks God made you to run on.